BUMPER BOOK OF un useless JAPANESE INVENTIONS

The Author Kenji Kawakami began his creative career in the Sixties writing scripts for animated TV series, and went on to arrange media events, becoming an avid opponent of such Japanese institutions as karaoke. After designing the Tokyo Bicycle Museum in the mid-Eighties, he became editor of a popular home shopping magazine, in which the concept of Chindogu was first born. The author of four books of unuseless inventions, and founder of the 10,000-strong International Chindogu Society, he is famous throughout Japan for his bizarre gadgets and his tireless work for the better understanding and appreciation of the tenets of Chindogu.

The Translator Dan Papia gave up a successful career as a financial journalist in 1991 to focus on more serious pursuits, and almost immediately created the so-called 'eye paddle' — a ball painted to look like an eye attached to an optician's chart paddle. He gave the Tokyo Dome its official name ('Big Egg'), and introduced Chindogu to the world outside Japan. He currently runs a video distribution business, writes a media column for the *Mainichi* newspaper and a humorous column for the *Tokyo Journal* and appears irregularly on Japanese TV.

The Editor Former *Punch* restaurant critic and *Sunday Telegraph* columnist, Hugh Fearnley-Whittingstall is a writer and broadcaster whose primary journalistic interest has been food. It was pursuit of the deadly Japanese delicacy fugu (or puffer fish) that first brought him to Japan. He has produced several documentaries for television, including *The Maggot Mogul,* about a scheme to build the world's biggest maggot farm.

BUMPER BOOK OF unuseless JAPANESE INVENTIONS

The Art of *Chindogu*

Kenji Kawakami

Translated by and additional text by Dan Papia
Edited by Hugh Fearnley-Whittingstall

HarperCollins*Publishers*

HarperCollins*Publishers*
77–85 Fulham Palace Road,
Hammersmith, London W6 8JB

www.harpercollins.co.uk

This paperback edition 2004
1 3 5 7 9 8 6 4 2

101 Unuseless Japanese Inventions
First published in Great Britain by
HarperCollins*Publishers 1995*
Copyright © Kenji Kawakami 1995
Introduction © Hugh Fearnley-Whittingstall 1995

99 More Unuseless Japanese Inventions
First published in Great Britain by
HarperCollins*Publishers 1997*
Copyright © Kenji Kawakami and Dan Papia 1997

The Authors assert the moral right to
be identified as the authors of this work

Kenji Kawakami is the founder and President
of the International Chindogu Society

ISBN 0 00 719288 6

Set in Helvetica
Typeset by Francesca Belanger

Printed and bound in Great Britain by
Scotprint, Haddington

Editor's Foreword

Genius has most satisfactorily been described as the infinite capacity to take pains. By this reckoning the creators of the carefully crafted Chindogu in this book must rank as genius every one. The fact that they often create more pains than they take adds an extra dimension to their brilliance.

The original genius and founder of Chindogu is Kenji Kawakami, designer, anarchist, pathological mail-order enthusiast, and author of this book. I met him in December 1993, on the last evening of a ten-day trip to Japan while writing some articles for the *Sunday Telegraph*. Kawakami's work was to have been the subject of one of those articles. But when he showed me the half-dozen Chindogu that were scattered about his profoundly untidy office (among them the Eye Drop Glasses and the Panorama Camera), and then produced three books with photographs of hundreds more mind-unbending inventions, I realised I had met someone who could truly speak to the world. An article, disposable and ephemeral, would not be enough.

As he demonstrated the solemn function of the Fish Face Cover and the Telephone Dumbell, his wide-eyed earnestness collapsed periodically into infectious giggling. And I began to glimpse the universal charm of these Chindogu (a word which is, you should note, both plural and singular – very singular). Designed to solve many of the niggling little problems of modern life, at home, at work, at leisure (and, incidentally, while commuting between the three) they have a tendency to fail completely – but also heroically, magnificently and beautifully.

For me, the best thing about Chindogu is that they are real: all the inventions that appear in this book have actually been made, painstakingly and skilfully, by Kawakami and fellow Chindogu enthusiasts in Japan. They are also surreal – in even contemplating their use you enter a new and uncharted dimension of human endeavour. And Chindogu are full of stimulating contradictions. They are at once gentle and subversive, anarchic and mundane, ingenious and stupid. Are they art? It probably doesn't matter. But it definitely matters that it probably doesn't matter.

At the end of my intoxicating first encounter with Chindogu, I enthusiastically agreed to help Kawakami bring his work to the attention of the English speaking world. Almost two years later, this book is the result. I feel that my contribution as editor may not at times have been entirely unuseless. But it has certainly been fun.

Hugh Fearnley-Whittingstall

INTRODUCTION

There are those who date the dawn of our species at the invention of the first tool. Perhaps mankind can be said to have originated the moment that a certain hairless and ambitious ape threw a stone at a deer and turned the tedious task of chasing and killing into a far less loathsome chore.

The primitive tools that have since punctuated the process of our so-called civilization - at least according to the history books - were all to some degree more advanced than the previous ones. But we can suppose that for every inspired notion that advanced the human situation, there must have been at least as many duds; ideas for improvement that didn't quite work. Another hairless ape, for example, maybe the brother-in-law of the first tool-making human, might have grown tired of eating deer and envisioned a huge hill-sized boulder flying through the air and downing a nice thick woolly mammoth, only to finally decide that the rock would be too hard to throw and the whole operation certainly more trouble than it was worth. You'd have to roll it up a mountain, wait for the right chance, hope the beast wouldn't move...

It is this second sort of idea – just as noble but fruitless and until now less appreciated – that the art of Chindogu was conceived to celebrate. The Japanese word Chindogu literally means an odd or distorted tool – a faithful representation of a plan that doesn't quite cut the mustard.

The successful Chindoguist approaches his subject in much the same way that a serious inventor would: searching for an aspect of life that could somehow be rendered more convenient and concocting a method for making it so. Like the inventor, he discards those notions that clearly miss the mark, but unlike the inventor, he also abandons those ideas that will obviously work. The Chindoguist latches onto and builds a prototype of the best idea he can come up with that looks good at the onset but on closer examination isn't. Having tested and verified that it indeed wasn't worth the effort, the creator of the Chindogu will then congratulate himself on having successfully produced an almost useful implement.

Chindogu are inventions that seem like they're going to make life a lot easier, but don't. Unlike joke presents built specifically to shock or amuse, Chindogu are products that we believe we want - if not need - the minute we see them. They are gadgets that promise to give us something, and it is only at second or third glance that we realize that their gift is undone by that which they take away.

They are funny because they are paradoxical and they are funny because they fail, but Chindogu are not designed to be stupid for the mere sake of stupidity. To believe this would be a grave error. They are exactly what we've always longed for without actually realizing it; they are inventions that do a job, satisfy a need; they are everything it takes to bridge the distance between what we are and what we could be...almost.

Unlike the hungry simian with his unfulfilled craving for mammoth meat, we children of the prosperous twentieth century have the luxury of being able to

build that which we can't really use. Separated from the realm of practicality and profits, from the constraints of utilitarian application, they can take us into a new and spectacular world of human invention whenever we are lonely, angry or depressed. All we have to do is adhere to the ten tenets of Chindogu to insure that the purity and integrity of the discipline is maintained, and the process of encouraging and preserving the almost inspired and nearly brilliant becomes an instinctive way of life. We can scarcely look at a coffee cup without wondering whether another handle would make it twice as easy to pick up (and, if so, shouldn't ten more increase the convenience tenfold?). Chindogu lends an ever present quality of anarchy to even our most common concerns and a new dimension to our earthly existence.

In simple 1990s' terms, the practice of Chindogu is like a Jurassic Park for those less fortunate of man's labour-saving dreams and schemes. The International Chindogu Society protects and nurtures those ideas that technological evolution would otherwise doom to extinction so that we can, at our leisure, observe them, admire them and enjoy them.

We hope this book will help you, too, to take part in and take pleasure from this new and exciting form of non-verbal communication.

The Ten Tenets of Chindogu

Every Chindogu is an almost useless object, but not every almost useless object is a Chindogu. In order to transcend the realms of the merely almost useless, and join the ranks of the *really* almost useless, certain vital criteria must be met. It is these criteria, a set of ten vital tenets, that define the gentle art and philosophy of Chindogu. Here they are:

1. A Chindogu cannot be for real use

It is fundamental to the spirit of Chindogu that inventions claiming Chindogu status must be, from a practical point of view, (almost) completely useless. If you invent something which turns out to be so handy that you use it all the time, then you have failed to make a Chindogu. Try the Patent Office.

2. A Chindogu must exist

You're not allowed to use a Chindogu, but it must be made. You have to be able to hold it in your hand and think 'I can actually imagine someone using this. Almost.' In order to be useless, it must first be.

3. Inherent in every Chindogu is the spirit of anarchy

Chindogu are man-made objects that have broken free from the chains of usefulness. They represent freedom of thought and action: the freedom to challenge the suffocating historical dominance of conservative utility; the freedom to be (almost) useless.

4. Chindogu are tools for everyday life

Chindogu are a form of nonverbal communication understandable to everyone, everywhere. Specialised or technical inventions, like a three-handled sprocket loosener for drainpipes centred between two under-the-sink cabinet doors (the uselessness of which will only be appreciated by plumbers), do not count.

5. Chindogu are not for sale

Chindogu are not tradable commodities. If you accept money for one you surrender your purity. They must not even be sold as a joke.

6. Humour must not be the sole reason for creating a Chindogu

The creation of Chindogu is fundamentally a problem-solving activity. Humour is simply the by-product of finding an elaborate or unconventional solution to a problem that may not have been that pressing to begin with.

7. Chindogu is not propaganda

Chindogu are innocent. They are made to be used, even though they cannot be used. They should not be created as a perverse or ironic comment on the sorry state of mankind.

8. Chindogu are never taboo

The International Chindogu Society has established certain standards of social decency. Cheap sexual innuendo, humour of a vulgar nature, and sick or cruel jokes that debase the sanctity of living things are not allowed.

9. Chindogu cannot be patented

Chindogu are offerings to the rest of the world – they are not therefore ideas to be copyrighted, patented, collected and owned. As they say in Spain, *mi Chindogu es tu Chindogu.*

10. Chindogu are without prejudice

Chindogu must never favour one race or religion over another. Young and old, male and female, rich and poor – all should have a free and equal chance to enjoy each and every Chindogu.

珍道具

The Lipstick Seal
✱ For ladylike smudgeless sipping

Ladies (and other lipstick wearers), your beverage consumption need no longer be marred by the ever present fear of leaving unsightly lip-prints on your drinking vessel. The lipstick seal is an adhesive stick-on transparent tab that will banish this inadvertent discourtesy from your life forever. Just peel off and throw away when the drinking hour is over, and the lip-contact portion of your glass or mug will still be pristine clean.

Lady's Coffee Mug
✳ The alternative lip-smudge avoidance device

$\mathbb{S}$hould the lipstick seal prove user unfriendly, or to avoid the necessity of carrying spares, the Lady's Coffee Mug will solve the coffee-break lip-print problem once and for all.

Based on the time-honoured principle of camouflage, the sipping area of the mug, both inside and out, is coloured lipstick red, rendering those lip prints invisible to social score-settlers and etiquette terrorists. And no used lipstick seals to clutter up the ashtrays.

The Forward-Backward Glasses
✳ For simultaneous front and rear vision

Recognise your friends before they surprise you from behind. Spot the long arm of the law creeping up on you. Anticipate those pushy pedestrians. With the left eye looking forward, the right eye back, you need never miss a trick.

Unfortunately human ocular evolution has not kept pace with such ingenious technology, and wearers of the Forward-Backward Glasses will struggle to achieve simultaneous front and rear vision. But don't be downhearted. Keep a pair in the family, and your great, great, great, great, great, great, great, great, great, great, great (and then some) grandchildren may feel the benefit.

Duster Slippers For Cats

✳ *For feline assistance with tedious housework*

Now the most boring job around the house becomes hours of fun. Not for you, but for your cat! With these dust-dislodging foot socks, cats can play their part in easing the pressure of domestic chores. Lazy cats are of course much less productive than excitable ones, but this problem may be overcome if you introduce a dog into the house.

The Telephone Dumbbell
✳ Increases fitness and reduces phone bills

Lazy kids never off the phone? Discourage lengthy phone calls and turn fat to muscle with the telephone dumbbell. The five-kilo standard model means that most calls will run under three minutes, but serious scrimpers may be interested in the ten-kilo phone, which brings average talk time down to a super-brisk, 'hello-goodbye' thirty seconds.

In the public domain, the Dumbbell Phonebox reduces waiting time and boosts national fitness.

Newspaper Bath Packs
✳ *Vinyl waterproofing for broadsheet newspapers*

Rubber ducks may be fun but they won't help you get ahead in the morning. Scientists have shown that a good hot bath stimulates alpha waves in the brain. So, for optimum use of bathtime, get your body clean and your brain ready for the day — read the paper in the bath.

One vinyl pack encloses four pages of news, counting the front and back. So, for a thirty-two-page section, only eight recyclable packages are required. And they don't just keep the water out, they keep the newspaper ink in. So no more cloudy grey papier-mâché baths.

The Noodle Eater's Hair Guard

✴ Helps rapid lunchers protect expensive coiffeur

The Samurai hairstyle may have been an ancient and artful solution to the problem of maintaining follicular hygiene at mealtimes. Fashion has changed, and this age-old problem has returned. The modern solution is the Noodle Eater's Hair Guard. In stylish candy pink moulded plastic it fits neatly into briefcase or handbag.

珍道具

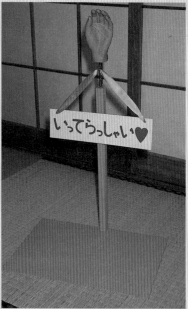

いってらっしゃい♥

Housewife's Snooze Aid

✳ Wave goodbye to housework fatigue

The exhausted housewife merits the occasional lie-in. But such indulgence can jeopardise marital bliss. How, for example, can the snoozing wife wave goodbye to her husband as he leaves for work? The answer is the Housewife's Snooze Aid, an automated waving hand, attached to an alarm clock, and timed to give a cheery wave just as hubby puts his head round the door to announce his departure. Hang the 'welcome back' sign underneath, and she can get away with sleeping the whole day through.

The Earring Safety Net

✳ Wherever you go, your earrings come too

T he loss of an earring can be sad, expensive, inconvenient – even incriminating (depending where the earring turns up). Don't let these negative forces spoil your day. Travel everywhere with your earring safety nets firmly in place – and don't forget to check them regularly.

Full Body Umbrella
✳ For day-long all-over dryness

The umbrella, invented over 200 years ago, was a good start in the technological battle to stay dry in the rain. But total victory has had to wait until now. Protected by a 360° sheet of clear vinyl, users of the full body umbrella are safe from even those sneaky, low-flying horizontal rain drops. And other pedestrians will appreciate the lack of dangerous spikes at eye level. Watch out for small dogs though.

Stretch Spoon
✳ Whenever that extra reach is needed

T he household spoon has evolved to its popular modern shape to serve most of our modern needs. But the one thing it just can't do is reach the bottom tenth of the average coffee jar. All too often the coffee maker is forced to improvise, and shake the last few spoonfuls from the jar straight into the cup. This slovenly practice leads to unpredictable beverage strength and reduced coffee break enjoyment. The Stretch Spoon brings relief. With its expanding telescopic handle it transforms from the regulation eleven centimetres to an impressive twenty-three.

Pant Hankies

✳ *A better life for impulsive hand wipers*

Too many of us are opting for a convenient but ultimately unsatisfactory piece of material on which to wipe wet hands — the seat of our pants. The upside, of course, is dry hands. But is it worth the downside — wet pants?

Of course, old habits die hard — so if you can't change the man, change the pants. Two thin strips of velcro on the seat of pants or skirt allow the wearing of detachable Pant Hankies. No need to curb the wiping instinct, and no more humiliating rear end rashes.

Fish Face Cover
✳ Helps get the fish cut up with minimum emotional trauma

Too many modern home cooks feel unable to look a dead fish in the eye. This has led to some nasty kitchen accidents, as the cook continues to slice with averted gaze. This in turn has given rise to the popularity of takeaway sushi and breadcrumbed fish fingers (you can buy five and shake them by the hand, but you still don't have to look them in the eye). In order that the art of fish cookery should not be lost forever, Chindogu brings you the Fish Face Cover. Slip it over the fish's head just prior to decapitation and avoid that reproachful stare.

Cat Tongue Soother
✳ *Food temperature control for cats*

Anyone who feeds their cat from the table will be aware of the feline aversion to hot food. In Japan this phenomenon is so familiar that people who have to blow on their noodles are said to have a 'cat tongue'. But sadly, owing to an evolutionary oversight, real cats can't blow on their food to cool it down.

They can now! This simple device allows cats to chill their chow with paw power. Now you can serve up piping hot food to your pet without fear of a visit from the Cat Protection League.

珍道具

Cranium Grabbing Glasses
✳ For short-sighted sideways snooozers

 $\mathbb{A}$ s anyone who requires corrective eyewear will tell you, the problem with wearing spectacles is not the lenses, it's the arms. And never more so than when you nod off during bedtime reading, or horizontal telly-watching. If you're not instantly woken by a jab behind the ear, then chances are you'll wake up with a one-armed pair of specs.

Banish such bother and breakages, with the sleep-safe Cranium Grabbing Glasses. Pilot wearers have complained of being laughed at. But are they really any less flattering? When the whole world has converted, we may decide not.

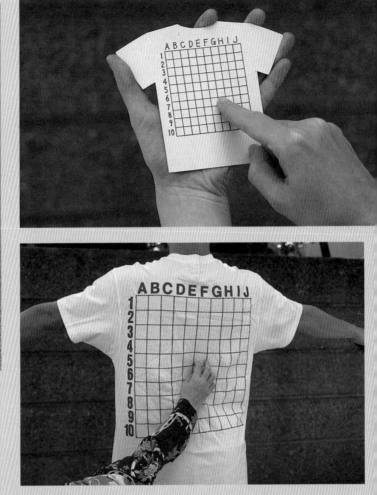

Back Scratcher's T-Shirt
✴ The fast and logical solution to infernal itching

The friend (or partner) who offers to scratch your back is a friend (or partner) indeed. Except it all goes horribly wrong when they just can't seem to locate the maddening itch. For those who are fed up of saying, 'left a bit …up a bit …right a bit …damn!' comes a very special t-shirt, complete with Battleships style, itch-locater grid. The scratchee is also equipped with a hand-held miniature corresponding grid-map, for accurate communication. So when the scratcher says, 'I'm scratching F5,' the scratchee can say, 'try G7'.

Handy Knife and Handy Cutting Board

✳ For hands-on food preparation

F or maximum control in a small space, and that invaluable feeling that one is completely in touch with one's produce, this complimentary pair of gloves constitutes a miniature portable food preparation system – both work surface and blade. Once you get used to them, you will hardly know where your body ends and your utensils begin. Not recommended for those who like to pick and nibble while they cook.

Personal Rain Saver

✳ *Every drop that falls is yours to keep*

No one has any illusions about the value of water as a natural resource. Yet all of us watch hundreds of gallons washing off our umbrellas and into the gutters every year. With the Personal Rain Saver you not only stay dry, you can collect your own share of natural precipitation in a shoulder-harnessed tank.

As an alternative to mass assembly, the Personal Rain Saver provides a pro-planet pastime for peaceful protestors to engage in on their own (weather permitting).

Soap Recycler
✶ *The answer to sud's law*

When a bar of soap is finally reduced to the little slippery slither that you just can't keep hold of, it becomes the scrimper's worst nightmare. You can't bear to throw it away, but you can't do a thing with it either. That's sud's law.

So save your slivers, until you have enough to fill your soap saver. Then turn the handle, and press the useless remnants into an all new bar of soap — quite possibly multi-coloured, multi-scented, and for all skin types.

Note: disturbing rumours have reached us that such a product is being marketed commercially in the US. Its status as Chindogu is there-fore under review.

Step Sandals

✳ The ultimate high heels

From earliest times, man has reached for the skies: hence the Tower of Babel, the hot air ballon and, at a more mundane domestic level, the step ladder. The latter is what most of us use to get a little lift in life, but it has its drawbacks – most obviously, when you move, it doesn't.

Step forward the step sandals, the latest in extendable tripod-fitted footwear. They provide artificial elevation with safe equilibrium. The domestic advantages are many: high dusting, ceiling painting, top bookshelf access. But you can also walk tall outside the home: see what the rest are missing when crowds gather and you're late on the scene. It also allows children to see the grown-up's point of view.

谷合

Shopper's Umbrella

✳ *Increases purchase power in a downpour*

For over a century now the umbrella has kept the rain off human heads, but at a price — one human hand. The committal of a full half of the carrying limbs to the business of holding the umbrella drastically reduces the ability of shoppers to carry the fruits of their acquisitional frenzy.

That's why the sturdy Shopper's Umbrella is fitted with eight hanging hooks attached to the canopy-supporting rods. These can be used to house and carry bags of all sorts, which will join you in the rain-free zone. Novices should beware of two small potential hazards: a poorly balanced umbrella and impaired vision.

41

Automated Noodle Cooler
✳ *Further assistance for the noodle-eater-in-a-hurry*

It is fundamental to Oriental cuisine that noodle soups are always served at a temperature at which they are infeasibly hot. The admirable reason is consumer choice; the diner can decide when his or her noodles have cooled sufficiently to be deemed palatable. But today, when time is money and money is scarce, not everyone can afford to wait around for noodles to cool. Frantic blowing is both undignified and limited in its effectiveness. The Automated Noodle Cooler is the answer. A compact fan, it fits tidily towards the holding end of one of a pair of chopsticks.

The Noodle Cooler can also be adapted to fit spoons and forks, and hence combat the problem of too-hot food as it arises in other cultures.

Butterstick

✳ *Why dirty a knife?*

Somewhere beyond the lipstick, gluestick and the stick deodorant comes the latest in stick-type-applicator-technology: the butterstick. Its manner of use is self-evident. Besides toast, it is useful for buttering corn on the cob and crumpets; less useful, unfortunately, for buttering rice and peas. Note also that, when cold from the fridge, the butterstick may have a tendency to 'flay' soft bread.

Soft Drink Holder

✱ *Even people with busy hands deserve refreshment*

T here are other devices that go by this name, but they are undoubtedly inferior. Why? Because they hold your drink not when you need it, only when you don't. The Chindogu Soft Drink Holder (plus extra-long Chindogu straw) gets drink to your mouth while your hands are more gainfully employed.

Shoe Tabs
✳ *Facilitate instant shoe removal*

Shoes that are reluctant to leave your feet can be a nuisance. Shoes that are very reluctant to leave your feet can be dangerous. Even if you succeed in prising off one shoe by using the heel of another, you have to put the first shoe back on again to get the other one off. And when you're hopping around, one shoe off, one shoe on, accidents can happen. Shoe tabs make all the difference. The shoe-less heel can safely and surely push on the tab to remove the shoe from the still-shod foot. But beware of striding confidently through a crowd, and finding yourself suddenly shoeless.

Sweetheart's Training Arm
✳ A PDA (Public Display of Affection) confidence developer

It's a tough life, these days, for a nervous or novice sweetheart – the kind of person who looks around at the young couples of today, strolling arm in arm and hand in hand, and thinks, 'I admire that bold statement of affection. But I'd never be able to do it myself.'

To the aid of such unfortunates comes this indispensible training device, a dummy arm. It attaches to a jacket or coat just next to the real arm. You can hold onto this simulated appendage in the early stages of courting, without the worry of sweaty palms, inappropriate pressure, or when to disengage.

Both male and female dummy arms are available, but it is advised that only the less confident partner of the couple attempts to train with the dummy arm. Otherwise a bizarre situation may arise, of doubtful benefit, in which one dummy arm is linked affectionately with another.

Ice Stopper

✳ **Protects the drinker's nose and lip from floating ice**

As everyone knows, ice floats. This means that the otherwise pleasurable activity of taking a drink on the rocks is fraught with the danger of ice cubes colliding with your nose and lip. With this washable, re-usable, one-size-fits-most-drinking-vessels ice-stopping net we can be freed from this anxiety at last. The Ice Stopper even protects from the most tiresome variety of face-ice collision: the last-sip sliding cubes syndrome that occurs when the base of an almost empty glass is raised above the horizontal.

珍道具

Eye Drop Funnel Glasses

✱ *For pupil-point accuracy*

Why is the application of eye-drops so problematic? You open your eyes wide, stare straight up at a bulging droplet, squeeze the bottle, and wait for gravity to do its job. Yet the next sensation you have is of the cool expensive medicine trickling down the side of your face. It's enough to make you weep.

These specially customized glasses guarantee no-more-tears eye drop application. No need for accuracy. Provided the solution makes it into the funnels, you'll score a bull's-eye every time.

Shoe Guards

❋ *Commuter resistant protection for well-shined shoes and sensitive toes*

In the twice-daily commuter crush, it's often your feet that come off worst. Even those fortunate enough to escape a toe-crushing can expect to lose the gloss on their well-buffed shoes. Now there is a dramatic but highly effective solution to both problems. Anyone incautious enough to step on these steel-spiked toe-guards will not make the same mistake twice.

If only Elvis had had a set, one feels his blue suede shoes would have been quite safe.

Lazy Grabber
✳ *The long arm that saves your legs*

It's all very well having labour-saving devices like the TV remote control. But what do you do when they stray out of reach? You sit and suffer until you have to get up for something really important anyway.

The lazy grabber alleviates such stress, by allowing you to retrieve such items without moving from the comfort of your favourite chair. It may, however, be advisable to have two Lazy Grabbers – just in case one of them strays out of reach.

Zip-up Cold Mask

✳ *For instant oral access*

The cold mask has long since shown its worth in keeping germs at bay. This popular accessory has, however, proved something of an inconvenience at mealtimes. The current options are either to remove the mask completely, thereby exposing yourself to foreign germs for the duration of your mealtime, or pull it down from the mouth for each sip or bite, causing uncomfortable elastic strain on the ears. As in so many areas of life, the zip fastener offers a simple solution. The Zip-up Cold Mask allows you to eat, drink, and even smoke, with minimal exposure to contaminated air.

SLIDE CLIF
BETWEEN LI
BEND BAC
AND SQUE
TO OPEN POU

Dear Everybody.

"A hamburger, eate

feeling blue, isn

're

Fresh Air Mask

✳ ***The natural remedy for bad city air***

W e all like to get out of the smoke for some clean country air. But for those who manage to escape less often than they'd like (practically all of us), there is another way. By bringing a living plant to your personal air space, the Fresh Air Mask ensures that Mother Nature has every opportunity to cleanse the air you breathe as only she knows how. A bonsai forest version of the Fresh Air Mask is currently in development.

Chin Switch

✳ For hands-free turning off and on

There are numerous occasions when the fingers may not be the best part of the body with which to turn on a switch. Perhaps they are unavailable (for example when you are carrying a precious work of art). Or they may be wet, or covered in sticky rice or tempura batter.

The Chin Switch is specially designed to be activated by one part of you that is almost certain not to be engaged in another task: your chin. Men who happen to be shaving will find that it is also easily activated by the elbow or forehead. Or finger.

Peanut Deshelling Bag
✳ You get the nut, the bag gets the shell

The peanut is a great treat, and never more so than when freshly sprung from its natural casing. The aftermath of a good shelling session is, however, the tidy housekeeper's worst nightmare. Bits of peanut shell find their way into the most unlikely places.

The Peanut Deshelling Bag may sound an unlikely enough place itself, but once inside it, nothing can escape – except the meaty kernel that is the true object of desire.

There are two openings for your hands, ample storage for a feast of nuts, and a clear vinyl window that allows you to keep an eye on your work. The bag is easily emptied after a session, but be careful not to spill shell fragments through the hand holes on the way to the waste bin.

Finger-mounted Toothbrush
* Oral hygiene at your fingertips

When it comes to perfect oral hygiene, there's one thing that always gets between you and your teeth – the handle of your toothbrush. We have removed this cumbersome impediment, and made toothbrushing a more hands on, or fingers on, experience. You can vary the pressure according to the sensitivity of individual teeth, and get in close to do more delicate work.

Author's note: Rumours have reached us that the fingertip toothbrush actually exists as a marketed product. If this is true, then it is technically disqualified from being a Chindogu. However, should the product fail to catch on and be withdrawn from the market, as we might anticipate, then its status as Chindogu may be restored.

Dust and Shake

✳ For well-earned after-chore refreshment

Y̶ou've heard of Shake 'n' Vac, but here's an even better way to put the freshness back into tedious household chores. Before dusting, fill the Dust and Shake with three parts gin, a dash of Martini, and half a dozen cracked ice cubes. Dust vigorously, then strain your chore-rewarding dry Martini into a glass, and put your feet up. Then get up, refill, and start on the next room. Your household chores will soon begin to seem like one long party.

Umbrella Tripod
✳ The photographer's friend come rain or shine

This essential aid for amateur photographers keeps the rain off your camera (in much the same way as a conventional umbrella), but when the sun comes out converts instantly to a stable tripod (strictly speaking an octopod, since the 'legs' on which it stands are the eight spokes of the umbrella's canopy). Ideal for those self-timer group shots, the Umbrella Tripod makes it even easier to smile for the camera.

Portable Stoplight

✳ Puts traffic control in the hands of those who need it most

Children do not always remember to apply the traffic safety code, and this is an increasing source of anxiety for parents. But now they can relax again – provided they have equipped their children with the Portable Stoplight.

The child in charge just switches it on and, regardless of whether he or she remembers to look both ways, a bright red light beams in both directions, halting the oncoming traffic. Despite its authentic design, the portable stoplight only shines red. The danger of carnage resulting from an accidental green light is thus cleverly avoided.

Magnetic Slippers

❋ Helps a pair stay a pair

How much time do we waste each year looking for a lost slipper? And how much distress is caused to fastidious members of society by the sight of two slippers not properly aligned, maybe even several feet apart? The deft use of a few small magnets has righted these wrongs. The slipper wearer simply clicks his or her heels together before taking off the slippers, and the pair remains in perfect togetherness until they are next put on. The slippers have the bonus function of picking up dropped pins and other small metallic objects as you walk around the house.

Vase Taps

❋ *Changes flower water quickly and cleanly*

Cut flowers rarely last as long as you hope, and one reason for this is certainly the tedious labour associated with changing the water. First you have to take out the flowers (which may have slimy stems), then throw away the old water, then fill the vase with fresh water, and finally replace the flowers. This is no doubt as stressful to the flowers as it is to you. The vase tap cuts these four difficult stages into two easy ones: empty, and refill.

It is particularly worthwhile to have a Vase Tap fitted to a priceless antique vase, as it greatly reduces the risk of breakage during a water change.

Table Groomer's Hand
✳ *Makes discretion the better part of oral hygiene*

A common problem encountered when dining in company is the small food particle lodged between the teeth. The traditional approach to this dilemma of social form is to attempt to remove the debris with the fingers of one hand, while masking your action with the other hand. This has never been satisfactory, as it leaves no hands free for the kind of social behaviour, principally eating and gesticulation, that would best disguise the unpleasant events.

So we bring you the Table Groomer's Hand, a moulded silicon facsimile which can be used to shield your clandestine cleaning activities. It is held up by a knob that fits between the fingers, yet leaves those same fingers freedom of movement to pick at the offending morsel. Meanwhile your third (real) hand is free for emphasis, coffee drinking, or playing games, whatever the occasion demands.

珍道具

Automatic Chew Counter
✳ No more too few chews

Today's food presents considerably less resistance to the teeth than that of our ancestors. Even the modern hamburger can practically be sucked through a straw. The consequence of this in the general population is lazy eating, ailing jaw strength and, when we do encounter foods that could do with a chew or two, indigestion. We know that a regime of proper chewing would rectify such problems – and an estimated 2,000 chews per meal is what the experts recommend. But who can be bothered to count?

The Automatic Chew Counter, that's who. Just strap it on at the beginning of a meal, and check the counter at the end. If you've fallen short of the requisite 2,000, then strap it back on and eat some more. Those on a diet are recommended to make up the deficit by vigorous 'air-chewing'.

Solar-powered Lighter
✳ *Light up while the sun shines*

Astroll in the park, a smoke on a bench – it's the perfect way to relax in your lunch hour. But stress and frustration come flooding back when you realize that your lighter is out of gas, and you've left your matches in the office. For the proud owner of the Solar-powered Lighter, all is not lost – provided the sun is shining. (In Britain, exclusive use of the Solar-powered Lighter is particularly recommended for anyone wishing to cut down their smoking habit dramatically.)

The Up/Down Toothbrush

✳ *Cuts brushing time in half*

With bristles running both ways, the logic of this labour-saving toothbrush is clear – only half the strokes are required to clean both top and bottom sets. The time-saving benefits are less apparent when the front and back as well as the ends of the teeth are taken into account. But at least the inside of your lips and the front of your tongue will also get a good clean.

Hay Fever Hat

✳ *The all day tissue dispenser*

Having hay fever is bad enough, but running out of hankies turns misfortune to misery. So, don't run out! The Hay Fever Hat supports a large loo roll, enough to cope with heavy blowing and incessant sneezing from dawn till dusk.

Portable Commuter Seat

Reserve a seat – take it with you

We all like to get a seat on a crowded train. But some of us don't want to fight for it (and some of us who do want to fight for it always seem to lose). As so often in life, the solution is to bring your own. The Portable Commuter Seat fits snuggly in the slight space between the thighs of more conventionally seated passengers. In fact the slighter the space the better the ride, as a tight fit means less wobbling will occur when the train goes round the bend.

Umbrella Shoe Savers
✳ **_Extends the life of expensive footwear_**

T he conventional umbrella offers proportionately decreasing protection from precipitation for the lower parts of the body. The latest in the Chindogu range of improved umbrella technology goes right where you need it most – on the long-suffering shoe. The mini-canopies have a full thirty-centimetre diameter guaranteed to keep the rain off the full front of foot area. Take off the umbrellas when you get where you're going, and your bone dry shoes look as good as they did when you put them on.

Note: the generous width of the umbrellas means that care must be taken when walking not to bring the feet too close together.

珍道具

Vanity Camera
✳ Allows last minute adjustments for the camera-shy

We all like to look our best for the camera. But who would trust a photographer to know when we look good? With its built-in mirror, the vanity camera gives the subject ultimate control. We can fine tune that smile, flatten stray hairs, and choose our best side, right up to the moment when the camera goes click.

Self-cooling Hat
✳ *Helps hot heads stay cool*

If you can't get ahead, get a hat.
But what can you get if your hat's too
hot? The Self-cooling Hat, of course.
The attached fan pumps out hot stale
air from inside the hat, and draws in
fresh cool air from outside the hat. It's
powered by a self-charging solar
battery, which stays on when the sun
goes in for a while, or the wearer
walks in the shade, but finally gives out
only when the cool air of the evening
has arrived.

Flotation Bag for Water Reading

✳ *Keeps the reader's head above water*

Having already solved the problem of reading in the bath (see page 16), Chindogu has taken on an even bigger challenge: the problem of reading while wading across large bodies of water. But why should anyone want to read while wading across large bodies of water? Because now they can!

With rubber boots attached to rubber trousers and an inflatable rubber ring, we've formed a waist-high underwater suit. In work or leisure clothes, you can get some relaxing float reading in at any time of day, and stay dry as a bone. And of course you don't have to wait till you encounter a body of water that needs to be crossed – you can do it for fun!

The Driver-drier

✳ *Improves the swing, dries the laundry*

Another two-in-one Chindogu labour saver, the Driver-drier not only does a fine practical job, it also goes a long way to restoring matrimonial harmony in households where golf widows have reached a point of despair. The golfing husband gets to practise his swing, while his wife has the satisfaction of finally seeing her partner contribute to the mountain of household chores.

Novice swingers should be careful not to swing those pristine whites too close to the grass, or the effect on matrimonial harmony may be swiftly reversed.

Subway Snoozer's Chin Stand

✳ Stand up for your right to snooze on the subway

Perhaps the last ditch alternative to the portable commuter seat (see page 76), this device allows even standing passengers the chance to score a few zeds in the rush-hour crush. It's a cushioned U-shaped chin rest mounted on an extendable steel stand. The Chin Stand can thus be adjusted to fit any body size, adult or child, from seventy-two centimeters to 187. Can also be taken to boring cocktail parties.

珍道具

Detachable Tooth Covers
* Saves brushing after every meal

After putting so much effort into a rigorous morning routine of dental hygiene, it can be distressing to find all that hard work undone by the midday meal. Detachable Tooth Covers put an end to contamination by food of pristine teeth. The gumshield-style silicon plates fit comfortably in the mouth and are easily attached and removed. Each plate is fitted with seven hygienic and hardwearing stainless steel artificial molars which allow you to crunch and chew without food coming in contact with your natural teeth. For those who like to keep their Detachable Tooth Covers in pristine condition, we are now developing Detachable Tooth Cover Covers.

Clean-up Slippers
✳ *Let nifty footwork do the housework*

Alittle piece of fluff or a scrap of paper on the floor hardly justifies wheeling out the vacuum cleaner, or even rushing to the cupboard for the dustpan and brush. But it is nonetheless unsightly, and a source of irritation to those who like to keep the house just so. Clean-up Slippers have a left toe-mounted mini dustpan and a right toe-mounted mini brush (reversable for the left-footed), which allow the wearer to deal with even the smallest blemish as it is encountered. This way a stroll around the house practically does the cleaning for you.

Note that any matter gathered in the dustpan should at once be disposed of in the rubbish bin, as by walking around after sweeping up, items of dirt can be redistributed inadvertently elsewhere in the house.

Self-stirring Frying Pan
✳ *Master of the stir-fry*

Up until now, the stir-fry gourmet has always required two instruments to pursue his or her culinary art: a frying pan, and a stirring utensil. The TV chefs make it look so easy, but in practice it requires a level of co-ordination beyond the ability of most home cooks. And that's why we built the Self-stirring Frying Pan. Its non-stick surface and rotating double spatula keeps your ingredients constantly on the move – all you have to do is turn the handle.

Cockroach Swatting Slippers
✳ *For longer range and greater accuracy*

Research has shown that the slipper is already the preferred instrument for indoor cockroach swatting, with up to eighty per cent of householders preferring indoor footwear to rolled up newspapers or paperback books. But why not improve your hit rate by investing in a pair of special Swatting Slippers? With telescoping handles you can operate from longer range with greater accuracy – no more desperate throwing of slippers as the scuttler disappears behind a sofa. Ideal for those who can't, or won't, get too close to their prey.

Perfect Cake Cutter

* For fair shares all round

Even the most fair-minded of hosts can come unstuck when dividing a round cake between a number of greedy guests. Dividing into two, four or eight is moderately easy to achieve by eye, six less so, and any odd number is simply hopeless. Someone's sure to feel short changed, and if kids are involved it's a no-win situation – unless you can persuade each of them that their bit is biggest.

The Perfect Cake Cutter transforms cake division into the happy family sharing situation it was always meant to be. This two-bladed device is attached to a 360º protractor, with one blade fixed on zero degrees and the other adjustable to create the required angle – 120º for a three-way division, 72º for five, and 51.4º for seven. Total fairness, of course, depends on being able to locate the exact centre of the cake, for which we suggest you use a compass and dividers.

Camera Umbrella
✳ *For rain-safe picture taking*

Wet weather might be threatening to spoil your holiday, but don't let it spoil your holiday snaps. This thirty centimetre dedicated umbrella fits into and over your camera, so that even if you get rained on, your camera doesn't. A second feature of this Chindogu is a special attachment that allows you to mount the camera on top of your own umbrella, so that both camera and camera operator remain dry. The camera thus mounted can even be operated by remote — though at the small price of rendering you unable to look through the viewfinder.

95

360° Panorama Camera
✳ For the all round view

A popular pastime amongst holiday photographers these days is the construction of the panoramic view. Conventionally this is achieved by taking one picture of the view, turning a little bit, taking another, until the complete view has been covered. It is, at best, an optimistic and inaccurate procedure which often yields patchy results. The Panorama Camera puts panoramic photography on an altogether more dependable footing. Seven outwardly pointing cameras are perfectly angled to ensure that all the pictures will fit together neatly. They are also fired simultaneously, a highly desirable feature which eliminates the embarrassment of having, for example, the same bird flying through two different sections of the panorama.

For maximum enjoyment of your panorama, tape the seven pictures together with the images facing inwards and place your head in the centre of the loop. Then revolve the loop slowly around your head.

珍道具

Orange Peel Thumbnails
✳ Restores comfort and dignity to orange eating by hand

The close-to-nature way to eat an orange is to break the skin with your thumbnail and use the same thumb to lever off strips of peel and pith till the fleshy segments are revealed. But with orange stains on your thumb, debris stuck behind your nail, and juice stinging any minor abrasions, it's a high price to pay for oranges *au naturel*. The Orange Peel Thumbnail is a robust rubber artificial thumb top with stainless steel nail. It fits over your natural thumb, allowing you to dig in to an orange with enthusiasm but without contamination. Nail-biters will also find it useful for opening penknives and scratching backs.

Wide Awake Eyeopener

* Keeps tired eyes open

When exams are looming, it often seems there aren't enough hours in the day to cram in all that vital information. So here's a way to turn sleeping time into waking and working time, without the use of caffeine or other stay-awake pharmaceuticals. Regular clothes pegs grasp the eyelids, which are held open by attachment to a head-fastener made from a rubber ring worn on the top of the head.

Those who have tried this Chindogu have complained of considerable pain – which suggests it is doing its job even better than we first thought.

No Bite Nails
✳ Makes not biting nails more fun

Most treatments for nail biting depend on what psychologists call negative reinforcement. For example, nasty-tasting nail polish is supposed to provide a strong disincentive for nail-nibbling. We prefer positive reinforcement: you can bite these stick-on nails to your heart's content. Made of seaweed, they're nutritious, delicious, and surprisingly similar in texture to real human nails. A satisfying chew which leaves your own nails to grow long and strong.

Portable Office Tie
✶ *The busy executive wins by a neck*

It seems somehow appropriate that that vital sartorial accessory of the businessman's uniform, the neck tie, should be put to practical use. For the real 'power tie' is not the one with the expensive designer label on it, but the one which allows you to keep ahead of business colleagues when away from your desk. The pockets and compartments of the Portable Office Tie will carry pens, business cards, calculators and notebooks – or can be customised to suit your particular line of business. It is recommended that the tie is not tied or untied until office stationery has been removed.

Earplug Earrings

✳ **Instant protecton from deafening discos**

This stylish jewelry has a well-disguised function. The attractive green pendants that hang from each hoop are in fact fully functioning rubber earplugs. Always ready, just where you need them, the earplug pendants are easily inserted without drawing attention to yourself – you can pretend you are simply adjusting your earrings. Thus you can block out the beat of blaring discotheques without being thought unhip, and turn off the sound of bossy boyfriends or too talkative teachers without being thought rude. And if anybody tells you your earrings look stupid . . . well, you don't have to listen.

Gossip Guard
✱ *Helps you think before you speak*

In a free flow gossip situation, even the most socially upstanding of us can find that we have let mischievous cats out of their bags. The Gossip Guard helps reduce damaging prittle prattle by giving you that extra moment of reflection in which to check the impulse to start wagging your tongue. The device comprises a pair of lips in comfortable hygienic polyester, with a zipper to keep the mouth closed. When, and only when, the wearer is confident that his or her proposed act of speech is free from malice or unreliable information, the zip should be opened and the words released to the waiting audience.

Nostril Plugs
✳ *Keep your nose clean – on the inside*

For hay fever sufferers this ingenious device might be seen even as an improvement on the Hay Fever Hat (see page 74). Each Nostril Plug contains an effective and replacable charcoal filter to keep out pollen, dust and other allergy-provoking particles. They are also very useful in the presence of talkative barbers with bad breath.

Faulty or damaged Nostril Plugs have their own self-disposal mechanism – one sneeze and they're gone.

Hair Plait Helmet
✳ *Safety first, coiffeur second*

In this age of sexual equality, girls want to ride mountain bikes too. But this shouldn't restrict them to a boyish hairstyle – even if this is the only kind that remains comfortable under a biker's helmet. In response to this dilemma, we devised this safety headgear especially for girls torn between their braids and their bikes. The fully cushioned safety helmet contains four holes specially placed to allow the release of long hair, particularly plaits. Note, however, that flying plaits may present an extra hazard in adventurous biking.

Straight-in-the-pan Chopping Board

* Facilitates board–saucepan transfer of chopped ingredients

Next to the favourite knife, the chopping board is perhaps the cook's best friend. But it can seem more like a worst enemy when, on the journey to the saucepan, bits of chopped vegetable start to leave the board and relocate on the floor, work surface, and cooker. With this specially designed board such involuntary dispersal should no longer be a problem. The board can be placed so that the hole is directly over the saucepan, and the chopped ingredients are steered into the hole. Far too useful to be a real Chindogu? Maybe, except that cooks may find that, before it reaches the saucepan, as a method of ingredient dispersal the board-with-a-hole far outshines the original on which it was intended to improve.

珍道具

Heavy Smoker's Mask

✳ **Why smoke one when you can smoke fourteen?**

With no-smoking on public transport, non-smoking offices and non-smoking restaurants, it can be tough to get a cigarette in at all these days. So when you do find an acceptable smoker's niche, you may want to make up the lost ground. The Heavy Smoker's Mask allows you to smoke fourteen whole cigarettes in the time it would normally take to smoke one. So even a sixty-a-day smoker need only take five cigarette breaks to more than satisfy his or her habit.

Lawn Sandals

✳ *Always walk on the grass*

Y ou can't beat the sensation of fresh green grass between your toes. But you can join it. The surface of the Lawn Sandals are covered with super-realistic artificial grass, to stimulate the soles and elevate the soul. You need never walk on tarmac or concrete again. Lawn sandals are fully washable, and guaranteed free of mud, moss and thistles.

Natto Cutters

✳ For less messy brecky

This device is a long overdue response to the problem posed by the famous Japanese breakfast dish, natto. This sweet, stringy, sticky foodstuff makes hot mozzarella look rigid by comparison. Lift natto with your chopsticks, and the strands just stretch and stretch. And when they do finally break, you can be sure they'll wrap themselves around your face, or cling to your clothes, leaving you with a persistent physical and olfactory reminder of what you had for breakfast.

Mounted on a one-size-fits-all bowl stand, the Natto Cutter allows you to select a manageable length of natto and snip it before it gets out of hand. Should bring peace of mind and reduced dry cleaning bills to natto lovers everywhere.

Portable Subway Strap
✳ **Don't give up, hang up**

Perhaps the simplest device so far devised in the imaginative commmuter-aid department of Chindogu. You haven't got a seat (not even a portable one – see page 76) and there isn't even room to unfold the Commuter's Chin Stand (see page 89). Worse still, all the straps are taken – except the one you keep in your briefcase. The Portable Subway Strap has a plunger-type sucker attached to one end that fastens securely to the roof of the train. The suction is just strong enough to take the weight off your feet, just weak enough to be removed with a firm pull when you reach your destination. And just useful enough to be the envy of your strapless fellow passengers.

Temporary Ladies' Room Converter

✳ **Stake your claim to the facilities**

In small restaurants and other public places where the best they can offer in the way of toilet facilities is a shared rest room, ladies in particular may find the arrangement unsatisfactory. In order to dissuade impatient men from coughing loudly outside the door and repeatedly trying the door handle, the Temporary Ladies' Room Converter will come in very useful. Just stick up the sign when the coast is clear and take all the time you like. And when you finally emerge, you can enjoy the sight of men wandering around in distracted ˆonfusion.

Multi-spicketed Watering Can
✳ *You can't make it rain, but you can make it pour*

Yet another application of the think in multiples branch of creative Chindoguing, the Multi-spicketed Watering Can greatly reduces irksome pot plant watering time. Nurseries and gardening centres can use it to reduce staff by seventy-five per cent. Note that pots should be carefully aligned, and also that greatest efficiency is achieved if the number of plants in your collection is divisible by four.

LADIES

115

珍道具

Golfer's Practice Umbrella
✷ *Work on your swing: swing on the way to work*

Men will be boys, and it's a common sight on the subway platform to see commuting golf enthusiasts practising their stroke with a furled umbrella. These besuited golfers tend not to impress however, bearing as they do a markedly greater resemblance to businessmen being eccentric with umbrellas than to sub-scratch handicap golf professionals. With a real driver head, the Golfer's Practice Umbrella is designed to improve both the performance, and the image in the eyes of critical fellow passengers, of these frustrated Nick Faldos. It is quite passably functional as an umbrella too, but is not recommended for use on a real golf course, as the user would look stupid.

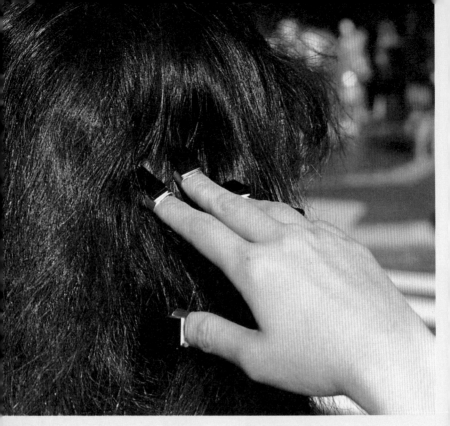

Finger Combs
✳ *For more discreet personal grooming*

Nobody admires the vain individual who produces a comb in public and begins restyling their hair. Yet what can you do on the way to a date or important meeting when you can't get to the respectable privacy of a cloakroom? Miniature Finger Combs provide a discreet reassurance on all such occasions. Slip them on and pretend to be scratching your head over a difficult crossword clue, or just running your fingers through your hair in a carefree manner. No one need know that in fact you are removing unsightly tangles, or reinstating a lost parting.

Hairy Ego Booster

✳ Leave home without hair, but with confidence

The bald man's pyschological dilemma is a complex one. To wear a wig or hairpiece would be to admit to friends and colleagues that your patial deficit bothers you. Yet wouldn't it be nice to look in the shaving mirror every morning and see a man with a lovely head of hair? Well now you can. The Hairy Ego Booster is an adjustable crop of real hair designed to stand between you and your shaving mirror to produce, by optical trickery, the illusion that you are in fact endowed with an impressive mane of thick locks. The result is reduced negative shaving mirror feedback and restored positive self image. You can leave the house each morning with a virile spring in your step. But be careful to avoid glancing at reflective or highly polished surfaces for the rest of the day

One Stroke Brush
✱ For instant grooming

Hair brushes have long been available in all sorts of shapes and sizes – except the obvious. So not before time we bring you ... the hairbrush that actually fits your head. The scalp-contoured One Stroke Brush allows you to brush a whole head of hair (your own or a friend's) with a single firm stroke. Mousses and styling lotions can also be more quickly and evenly incorporated.

The Velcro Home Jogger
✳ The economic alternative in home fitness

Why pay for an expensive powered jogger's treadmill, when a little Chindogu ingenuity can give you a full jogging workout for a fraction of the price? Shod in special trainers soled with male 'hook' velcro, the exerciser jogs on the spot over a specially designed mat of female 'loop' velcro. The interaction between the two velcro surfaces produces sufficient resistance to require considerable physical effort. Ambitious indoor joggers may wish to consider carpeting their entire house with loop velcro to vary the available jogging landscape, or keep fit while they do the housework.

Vertigo Soothing Glasses
✳ Keep solid ground in sight

Today's high-rise office blocks can strike terror into the hearts of the vertigo suffering salaryman. So what do you do when career advancement means a move to the fortieth floor? The Vertigo Soothing Glasses can't bring you back down to earth, but they can bring the earth up to eye level, for that comforting 'close-to-solid-ground' feeling.

Note: some vertigo sufferers may find the problem of not being able to see their own feet a high price to pay.

Golf Hoe
✱ *Drive out weeds, literally*

Another two-in-one Chindogu which allows the user to combine two of the most popular modern hobbies, golf and gardening. It takes a few well-timed swings to purge the lawn of a stubborn clump of weeds, and in so doing you will strengthen your golfing muscles and improve hand-eye co-ordination. The added bonus is that there is no need to replace divots (though this is not a habit to be carried on to the country club).

珍道具

The Geta Shoe
✳ Combined Occidental-Oriental footwear for men

As East meets West in the business centres of the world, when it comes to formal business attire, the West has undoubtedly prevailed. The tunic and kimono have been supplanted by the pinstripe suit, and the traditional Geta sandal by the moccasin and the brogue. But homesick Japanese country boys, and Westerners who would like to sample the sensation of old style Oriental footwear, can take solace in the Geta shoe. As it keeps up Western appearances, it is sure to be acceptable in the business community. But the physical sensation of walking on these shoes is akin to hobbling along on a dirt road on the way back from the bathhouse.

Finger Protector
✳ *For dangerous and dirty manual tasks*

This silicone substitute hand is designed to reduce the danger of cutting your own fingers when preparing food. Careless choppers can become carefree, slicing away at high speed, safe in the knowledge that damage done will be to a hand that doesn't mind. It won't recoil from dirty jobs either, so if you happen to be phobic about raw onions, fish scales, or the slippery vegetable debris that collects in the plug of the kitchen sink, then allow fearless silicone fingers to lend a hand.

Umbrella Head Belt
✴ When it starts to rain, use your head

Another Chindogu to increase the range of activities available to the user during inclement weather, the Umbrella Head Belt can be used to adapt most conventional umbrellas for hands-free use. By strapping the umbrella stalk to your head, the belt makes both arms available for carrying shopping, suitcases or large pet dogs that don't like the rain. Some co-ordination and balance, not to mention neck strength, are required for successful deployment. When it's windy as well as wet, use of the Umbrella Head Belt is certainly not recommended.

Walk 'n' Wash

✳ *Makes washing day a stroll in the park*

Some choices are hard, especially when guilt enters the frame. You'd like to go for a walk, but you ought to be doing the laundry. Well now you can do both. The Walk 'n' Wash comprises a pair of polythene tanks, one for each leg, with the capacity to hold two litres of laundry and water. So it's wash on the right leg, then rinse on the left (or vice versa, according to your personal preference). The weight of the tanks turns walking into a workout, making this a triple-barrelled Chindogu.

Daddy Nurser
✳ *Lets Dad experience the joys of motherhood*

The division of work and responsibility within the modern family is constantly up for revision. Yet there is one task that still falls inevitably to the mother: breast-feeding the infants. This Chindogu challenges one of the last bastions of sexual inequality, and allows Father to experience the joy of nourishing his baby from his own body – almost. If this device was adopted on a large scale, then the benefits in terms of father–child bonding and the feminisation of the male could produce greater love and understanding on a global scale. Maybe.

Umbrella Drip Collector

* Protects floors from intrusive rainwater

Umbrellas are very good at keeping the rain off us when we are outdoors, but by a curious paradox they are also uncannily successful in bringing surprising quantities of rainwater indoors. The simple solution is the Umbrella Drip Collector – an inverted cup that attaches to the top of the umbrella. When the umbrella itself is inverted for temporary storage, the cup is the right way up, and well placed to catch the inevitable trickles. When you open the umbrella again, the collected water will run down the canopy and off into the gutter. (The old adage about not opening umbrellas indoors becomes particularly salient with this Chindogu.)

Hot Sake Bath Cup Holders
✳ *Makes sake drinking good clean fun*

Hot water is a resource too precious to waste on the unnecessary luxury of a long, lingering bath – which then goes down the plug hole. For greater energy efficiency, why not harness the heat of the bath to warm a few cups of sake? These sake cup-sized stainless steel sieves are suspended from miniature floating rubber rings, and are just deep enough to give maximum immersion to a near full cup of sake.

It is recommended that sake cups are placed in the holders after you have finished soaping. Careful bathers who do not splash too much may then enjoy a warm sake while they rinse.

135

珍道具

Portable Zebra Crossing

✳ **The pedestrian's best friend**

The tyranny of the automobile makes life increasingly tough for eco-conscious pedestrians, and finding a safe place to cross can result in inconvenient diversions and wasted time. Now the pedestrian can fight back. When you've found the crossing point that best suits you, simply roll out the the Portable Zebra Crossing in front of you and cross confidently and in safety at your own pace.

Warning: on busy roads where there is no break in the oncoming traffic, attempting to roll out the Portable Zebra Crossing can be hazardous.

Drain Cleaning Boots

* Makes light work of a heavy job

Inadequately cleaned drains and gutters can harbour filth and disease. Cleaning them out has never been a pleasant task, or one you would want to get your face or hands too close to. Well now you don't have to, because this sturdy pair of rubber boots is fitted with a fork and trowel — all you need to clear debris and establish a free flowing drain again. Once it was the least favourite on the list of family chores, but now they'll be queuing up to give the Drain Cleaning Boots a go.

睡眠中

新宿 ⇌ 八王子

Subway Sleeper's Screen
✳ *For more efficient sleep stealing*

The extra few minutes of sleep to be gained on the subway to and from work can be a valuable boost to your natural bedtime repose, but at what cost to personal dignity? Exhausted commuters are frequently seen slumped in their seats, legs apart, mouths open, snoring loudly. The Subway Sleeper's Screen addresses several anxieties of the underground snoozer, promoting a deeper, more refreshing sleep. Firstly it conceals his or her identity, hides an open mouth, and even goes some way towards muffling the sound of snoring. Secondly it masks the area that would be in view if the sleeper has fallen asleep with legs wide apart. Thirdly, the screen is emblazoned with the name of the station where you need to alight, so helpful (and appreciative) fellow passengers can wake you up in time.

Training High Heels

✳ Smooths the transition to adult female footwear

The graduation to high heels is something a young girl looks forward to as much as make-up and boyfriends. But when the big day comes, it can be frightening to mount those tottering towers and learn to walk all over again. An uncertain or lacklustre performance defeats the whole purpose of these elegant accessories. For beginnners, therefore, we recommend the Training High Heels. With miniature stabilising wheels attached to the pointy heels of either shoe, you can walk without fear of tipping over. When confidence and poise have been achieved, the wheels are removed and the young graduate can go solo.

Ten-in-one Gardening Tool
✳ *The amateur gardener's do-it-all*

The multi-faceted Swiss Army penknife is one of the great life-enhancers of modern times. By way of a tribute to the genius of this invention, Chindogu has moved the concept forward, and up in scale. The result is the Ten-in-one Gardening Tool, incorporating two sizes of shovel, a hoe, a blade, a saw, a set of pruning shears and several other gardening implements, all in one (moderately) compact unit. No more endless trips to and from the shed, and when the day's work is done, you won't have to remember all the tools you've scattered around the garden. However, you may want to think twice about lending your hoe to a needy neighbour, as everything else will have to go with it.

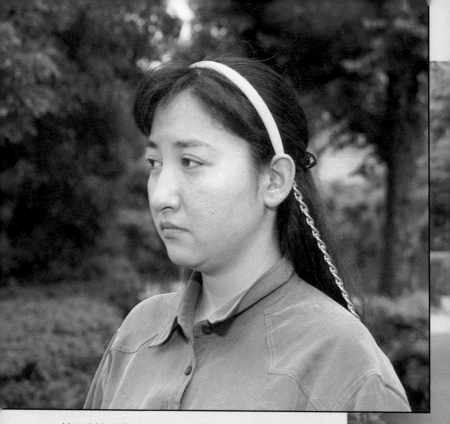

Head Handle for Shoulderbags

✱ For a more balanced approach to shopping

In just a morning tramping round the shops, a heavy handbag can play havoc with our physical equilibrium, causing shoulder pain, and back ache. So give the shoulder a rest: use the Head Handle to convert your handbag to a headbag. An attractive gold chain connected to a deceptively sturdy headband promotes more symmetrical distribution of weight. When you start to get a pain in the neck, you can revert to the traditional shoulder position.

Lawn-mowing Sandals

✳ *Labour-saving garden footwear for the supremely idle*

The prevalence of back yard jungles is a testament to the reluctance of the urban male to get round to mowing the lawn. The Lawn-mowing Sandals are designed to lure the reluctant mower back into the garden. Each has a miniature scythe protruding from the heel, so that even those who prefer a leisurely stroll to heaving a lawn mower up and down the yard can still get the grass cut. The steady shuffle of the truly indolent is more effective than vigorous striding up and down, which can have a tendency to take the blades over the top of the grass.

Outdoor Loo Seat
✱ Brings the great outdoors to the smallest room

For many people, lavatory time is leisure time, time for meditation and making peace with a hostile world. There's a lot to be said for improving the quality of this valuable time, and what better way to do it than by bringing nature even closer in this most natural of communions? The Outdoor Loo Seat is covered with convincing artificial grass that puts you instantly in touch with the wilderness. Piped birdsong and running water sounds will further enhance the experience, and those looking for true authenticity might consider sprinkling a few ants amongst the blades of plastic grass.

Balance Training Sandals
✳ *Improved co-ordination for the careless and clumsy*

Accident-prone types will be encouraged to learn that they can improve their equilibrium, and hence reduce the frequency of accidents caused by poor co-ordination. The road to success is to be walked wearing these unusual sandals. The inverted domes are exactly at the centre of gravity for the feet. The sandals are therefore hard to stand still in, but balance, and therefore confidence, are improved with walking. With practice the user will find that they can slow down, and even stop. By this time their balance, co-ordination, and accident rate will be the envy of all who once dared to call them clumsy.

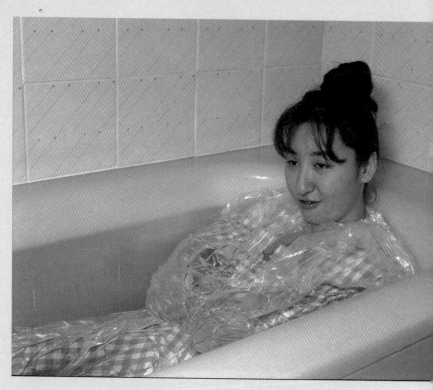

Hydrophobe's Bath Body Suit

✳ **Take a bath without getting wet**

The dry shave has already saved millions of man hours the world over. The dry bath is an even more radical concept, with the potential for even greater impact on the way we live. The benefits are considerable. No need to undress. No need to dry, talc up and redress. You can experience all the warmth, comfort and therapeutic relaxation of the conventional bath, without the wetness. You can then get out of the bath, surrounding yourself with the cool air of the bathroom, without the unpleasant chill factor that so often spoils the end of bath experience for the wet and naked.

Such is the pleasure and convenience of the dry bath, that wearers of the body suit may be inclined to 'soak' for very long periods. This is to be discouraged, as resulting excessive perspiration may require the remedy of a conventional wet bath.

151

ただいま眠っております。
お手数ですが下記の駅で
起こしてください。

西荻窪　多謝

ただいま眠っております。
お手数ですが下記の駅で
起こしてください。

西荻窪 多謝

Commuter's Helmet

✳ **For secure subway snoozing**

Another Chindogu to aid the comfort and repose of weary commuters, and arguably the best. Like the Subway Sleeper's Screen (see page 143), the Commuter's Helmet sports a message to fellow travellers, reading, 'I'm having a short nap. Could you please wake me up when I reach the stop printed below. Many Thanks.' But since it depends entirely on the co-operation of fellow passengers for success, this Chindogu has also been designed to maximise their finer communal instincts and sense of goodwill. The suction pad on the back of the helmet keeps the head firmly in place, thus preventing the sleeper's head from lolling intrusively on the shoulders or laps of his or her neighbours. This courtesy will no doubt be appreciated, and the reciprocal favour of a timely awakening is more likely to be achieved.

Drink De-carbonator
✳ Curbs troublesome bubbles

When daily after-work drinking is an offer you can't refuse, the strain on the stomach of the congenial salaryman can be too much to bear. Apart from alcohol itself, the gas in beer and carbonated mixer drinks is perhaps the prime culprit in professional dispepsia. Clearly we can't dispense with the alcohol; but we can, at last, dispense with the gas.

When a bubbly beverage is placed in the utility cup of the Drink De-carbonator, the switch activates high-powered vibrations which awaken the gas molecules and hasten their natural upward departure. Beers and gin and tonics are quickly rendered flat, and thereby less irritating to sensitive stomachs. Alcoholic drinks can be consumed in greater quantities, and the drinker can then focus his attention solely on the problem of inebriation.

Automobile Parasol
✻ *A cool car for a cool head*

On a sunny day, we'd all like a cool shady parking spot. But we rarely succeed in finding one, and the result is a hot car, steaming kids, melting pets – and inevitably a scorching temper on the part of the driver.

So if you can't park the car in the shade, park the shade on the car. The automobile parasol is over a metre and a half in diameter, and casts a big enough shadow to accommodate even a large family saloon. Can also be used in very slow traffic jams.

珍道具

Stormy Sky Tie

✴ *A must-have garment for wicked weather*

When you've got to lug an umbrella around just because the weathermen predict the chance of showers, you feel like you're getting the short end of a hook-tipped stick. And, if it doesn't rain, you'll probably leave it in a taxi.

The solution: an umbrella around the collar in the form of a tie. If you need it, it's there. And if you don't, you're still getting some use out of it. As a bonus, the added weight stops the tie blowing over your shoulder in a storm and it's lighter to carry than it would be at hand level.

Only one small Chindogu snag remains. When the umbrella is put into action, it makes for a wet shirt and suit when it reverts back to being a tie. But don't worry! If you never had the umbrella in the first place you'd have got wet anyway.

Portable Armrests

✳ With these in place, life's one big armchair

At the end of a hard day, luxury is a cushy recliner with padded armrests. Dining-chair uprights just don't give the same relief. So if fifty percent of that easy feeling is down to laid back arms, give your biceps a break even when walking. With Portable Armrests walking has never felt so good. While your legs take the strain, and your shoulders complain, your arms will be in paradise.

Rotating Spaghetti Fork

✳ *Takes the nuisance out of noodle nibbling*

The inventor of the tradition of eating spaghetti with a fork must have been a real practical joker. How is it possible to eat spaghetti and retain your dignity? At long last, the Rotating Spaghetti Fork is the answer.

With two small batteries and a motor that doesn't spin too fast in your utensil, you can turn pasta consumption into a smoother and more enjoyable enterprise.

✳ Give the appearance of paying attention

Want to sleep through lectures? Want to look alert rather than inebriated after lunch? Drooping eyelids giving the game away? From any teacher's or employer's point of view, you'll always be the most bright-eyed and bushy-tailed person in the room with Seeing Eye Seals. In fact, your educators and employers would probably love to have some of these themselves.

And, just think, on camping trips tigers won't sneak into your tent if they think you're awake. A pair of these could ward off everything and everyone – pests, pickpockets and policemen. We just don't recommend driving in them.

Face Ping Pong
✳ Give your head a workout

The challenge of designing a new international sport presented itself to us and, rising to the occasion, we came up with Face Ping Pong. The rules are simple. Keep your hands at your sides and bring the racket to the ball using only your head. Like most popular sports, the participants get to enjoy stimulating activity which they don't normally have the chance to indulge in, i.e. hitting things with your face. You'll find it every bit as fun and challenging as football or tennis and you will be sweat-soaked in next to no time. It's great exercise, but be prepared for a stiff neck the day after.

Last Bite Bar
✳ **The elegant way to clear your plate**

How many times could you have got away with using just a single fork or spoon were it not for that elusive last bite? When almost all your food is eaten and there's nothing left to use as leverage, you either need more silverware or to create a very smart diversion. The limitations of traditional cutlery mean that all too often diners are forced to submit their plates to waiters, bidding tearful farewells to those missed nibbles.

Those bites add up, so take what's rightfully yours and put hunger on hold. The Last Bite Bar can deliver that final dollop to your mouth.

Gift of the Gab Glasses
✳ A social leg up for the strong silent type

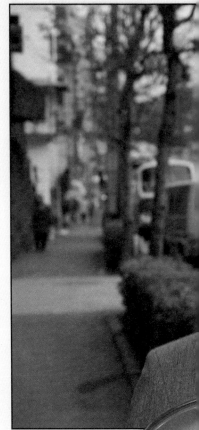

Some people just aren't good at talking, and the problem is that, despite the technological revolution, speech is still the most popular form of communication.

If you're shy or silent, don't put yourself at a disadvantage. Our Gift of the Gab Glasses enable even the most tongue-tied talker to give his audience the impression he's said at least three times as much as he actually has. But that's not all. They also render the listener speechless, making the wearer's conversation seem all the more skilled.

Walking around in these can be difficult, and glancing into a mirror downright scary. But it's good to talk.

珍道具

Shin Shines

✳ Give shoes a glow, even on the go

Shiny footwear speaks volumes. But the rub is that when you're an accomplished businessman there simply isn't time to rub your shoes. Shin Shines iron out this irony. At the bus stop or in the boardroom, brush-brush, wipe-wipe, and your shoes are again ready to attest to your success.

For the time being, ladies will just have to rely on the old trick of having closets full of extra shoes.

Extra Step Slippers
✳ A ten-centimetre lift – at the drop of a cup

When tall people need to be shorter, they can stoop. But unfortunately this simple theory doesn't work in reverse. The smaller members of our species are constantly having to appropriate ladders in order to reach things that are tantalizingly out of reach.

Get even with Extra Step Slippers. These light-weight booster cups are always poised to snap into place when an extra lift is needed. Walking in them may be uncomfortable, but so is a permanent stoop.

Four-for-One Floral Enhancer
✽ Saves money and space and looks great!

Longing to fill your home with the fancy floral arrangements found in glossy home decorating magazines? Strapped for cash? Dubious about the longevity of your blooms and unhappy with artificial alternatives? Make your flowers worthwhile. Three roses make a dozen when the Floral Enhancer is in place.

Business Tool Belt
✳ Everything you need for the office – in one place

Telephone repairmen and electricians get to carry all their important tools around their waist and are always poised for action. The average businessman has to make do with jotting down a note whenever he gets the urge, then waiting until he's back at the office. Not any more. With the Business Tool Belt name cards, telephone, calculator, bank slips and address book can be kept close at all times. The Business Tool Belt can get a little heavy, but maybe that's how repairmen stay in such good shape.

Wheels Wherever

✳ Removable rollers get things going

Some things are so heavy the manufacturers build them on rollers: filing cabinets, fridges, suitcases – objects we wouldn't be able to move any other way. Now see what wonders wheels can do for all those lighter objects too.

With adhesive-topped roller sets, just peel the seal and add a wheel. Make your household fully mobile. 'Where's the dictionary?', 'Could I have the mustard?' – just roll it over or pass it with a push. A word of warning: try not to think about what might happen in an earthquake.

Wide Angle Glasses
✳ Make tiny apartments into castles

Ⓢky-high rents in large cities make it impossible for the average person to have more than a room or two. The estate agent's spiel about 'One Room Mansions' sounds appealing, but your flat will still have about as much space as a rabbit hutch.

That's where Wide Angle Glasses come into their own. Like looking through a front door peep hole, with these on, the other side of a ten-foot room seems simply miles away.

Battery Free Mobile Phone

✷ *No charging, no phone bills, no worries*

It's easy to forget that the simplest solutions are always the best. Private calls on cellular waves are often hacked into by eavesdroppers; important information is at risk. Avoid all this hassle by saying no to portable phones.

With twenty feet of hose, the Battery Free Mobile Phone has plenty of scope to allow cost-free communication between two apartments in the same building, even two cars on the same road. There are no batteries, so you don't have to charge it up and there's no static, so you don't have to yell.

珍道具

Lipstick Guard

✳ **Protects your lips and other people**

It's bad etiquette to leave lipstick marks on people, especially those you don't know. But in crowded trains and cramped lifts, it can be hard to avoid close encounters. Try the Lipstick Guard for size.

With a discreet air hole to allow breathing, speaking, even smoking, the Lipstick Guard will not only protect the lips of the wearer, it also allows you secretly to chew gum or sleep with your mouth open without causing offence (provided you don't snore, of course).

One Cut Clippers

✳ *Don't like cutting your nails? One snip and it's all over*

⨍f you have an intolerance for the menial chores of personal grooming, this is the perfect short-cut for you. One Cut Clippers trim all the nails on a single hand in one fell swoop, with the added perk of cutting them all the same length. Flip it over and another clip tidies up the other hand. Easily adjustable, one set lasts a life time.

But hold your hand too far one way and you'll miss a nail. Hold it too far the other and you'll get part of your finger too. And don't forget: if you like having all your digits, adjust to the exact size of your hand or foot before use.

Aroma Eater

✳ *Dieting's a snap when everything smells so good*

The problem with healthy eating is that nutritious, good-for-the-body food just isn't exciting.

Since when did overweight people, struggling to take off the pounds, crave low-calorie food? Where's the fun in a lettuce leaf and a poached egg? After day three of your diet you never want to see another green bean again.

Working on the simple principle that smell accounts for a large proportion of taste, the Aroma Eater is the answer to the dieting dilemma. For the same reason that cup cakes don't taste nearly as good when eaten next to paper mills, bland, healthy foods are likely to go down a lot better when the eater is bombarded with the aromas of cocoa, cinnamon, bacon grease and parmesan cheese.

Solar Powered Flashlight

✳ For the visionary environmentalist

ispense with batteries. Take one solar panel and a torch and see how easy it is to harness light from the sun, converting it into six volts of pure power and a bright beam.

Brilliant, economical, effective, innovative. This archetypal Chindogu would be so completely useful were it not so completely useless.

Cranium Camera
✳ Keep ahead of the crowd

How many times have you stumbled upon a scene you've wanted to capture on film and not had your camera to hand? With the Cranium Camera there's no longer any need to lament its absence. It's always ready to shoot in an instant. With it strapped unobtrusively to your head, it goes without saying that you'll never leave your camera behind again.

Wrist Camera

✳ **When you need a camera...and quick**

Consider the wristwatch. If you can wear a clock on your wrist, then logic asks why not a camera? The Wrist Camera keeps your hands free and your camera on standby. At the drop of a hat, and the flick of a wrist, you can snap the perfect snap. If you're a spy, or maybe a paparazzi photographer and discretion is necessary, you can simply slip your hand in your pocket.

Extra Fingers

✳ *If maths isn't your strong point, you can count on these*

Mental mathematical blocks are a serious business. A lack of numerical prowess may result from a pathological dislike of your maths teacher, or from a debilitating crush on her. Alternatively, you may be a compulsive doubter and no matter how many times you're assured that six plus nine is fifteen, you just can't be sure. And why should you be when you only have ten fingers to count on?

Each block of Extra Fingers adds another fifteen digits to your arsenal (five plus five plus five – trust us). This way you can happily calculate small amounts on your fingers and physically see them add up.

Everywhere Exerciser
✴ Sitting, walking, standing, lying, eating...bench pressing

Allegedly, being a sports - man is a twenty-four-hour job. The same is true of a Chindoguist. So, luckily for athletes the world over, the Everywhere Exerciser is an indispensable workout machine for the bathroom, bedroom, work-room, waiting room, conference room, and even for destinations in between.

For business people who don't get enough exercise, including bank clerks looking to improve their figures, the Everywhere Exerciser is a workout tool that straps around your chest so that you can never 'accidentally' leave it somewhere. You'll be exercising in restaurants, trains and on the street. Now, unfortunately, there's no excuse.

Lean Prevention Gloves

✳ **Gloves that make sure you keep your chin up**

Sit at a table and before you know it you'll be tempted to rest your head on your hand. The next step is leaning over, falling asleep, or ruining your posture so that you wind up with a sore back and a stiff neck.

Lean Prevention Gloves solve all of the above by nipping the problem in the bud. If you slip up and let your impulse to lean get the better of you, chances are it won't happen again. It's been tested.

珍
道
具

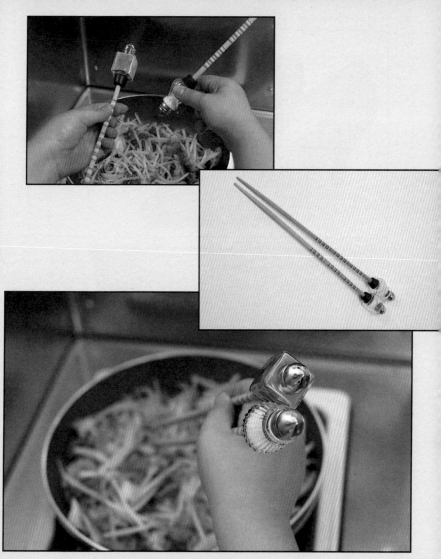

Cooking/Seasoning Chopsticks

✻ Do more for your dishes with less effort

Stir-fry cooking is quick and easy. One fire, one pot and, if you're eating alone, no dishes. Could anything be simpler? Yes. Now you don't even have to reach for the salt and pepper. They're at the end of your chopsticks! And if the food isn't spicy enough for your taste, adding more is easy to do — even while you eat.

Nature Lovers' Footwear

✳ For natural soles

It's hard to be a naturalist and a working professional at the same time. You want to be lying nude against a tree, but your boss wants you at a desk in a three-piece suit.

By wearing Nature Lovers' Footwear, your shoes will allow you to compromise. Commune with nature with each step you take, earn that executive's salary, and keep your freedom as your little secret.

Watch out for broken glass and soggy chewing gum.

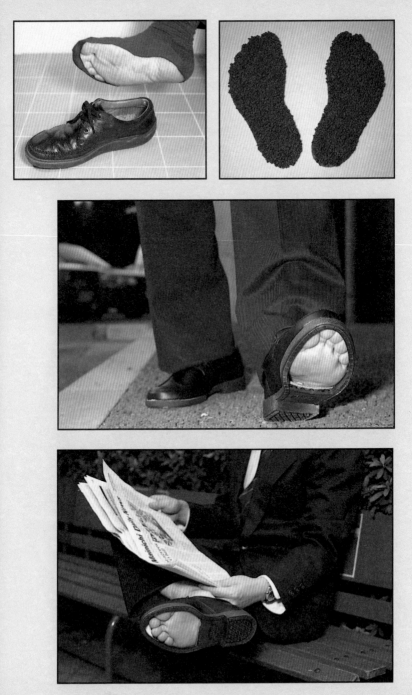

Everything Apron

✳ Want to be Queen of the Kitchen?

The art of good cooking is the delicate balance between art and science, and access to the right tools. Why settle for an apron with just one or two pockets on the front? The handier the tools, the better. Dress for action like any true technician. The Everything Apron brings the scouting notion of being prepared into the realm of gourmet.

Now you can cook more quickly and proficiently, with all you need just a hand's length away. And, with the added benefit of being the only one in the kitchen who can get to the tools, you'll never again suffer from too many cooks spoiling the broth.

Paint-on Plate Protector
✳ Takes the wet out of washing-up

Lots of people love to cook, to lay their creations out on elegant china, then devour them. That's the fun part, but few enjoy washing up afterwards. With a bottle of Paint-on Plate Protector, you don't have to any more. If you've layered your plates before laying out your food, cleaning up is merely a matter of lifting the protector and dumping the remains. The plates are as good as new and ready to be used again.

Tongue Cover

✳ **Take the heat off your tongue**

Tongues aren't always attractive but, boy, are they useful. They help us taste, talk and tease. But when you're really hungry and your food's really hot, they tend to get in the way. But not if you're wearing the Tongue Cover. Now you can shovel away fiery curry after steaming soup after boiling coffee and satisfy your stomach without harming that sensitive tongue. Possible drawback: you may find that your taste buds are a little less receptive.

珍道具

1

Personal Wake Up Headphones

✳ *Rouses the deepest of sleepers...in stereo*

Can't seem to get out of bed in the morning? No response to alarm clocks that beep, buzz or play music, snooze alarms that go off every few minutes, timers that turn on lights? When nothing else works, it's time to wake up, smell the coffee and get some Personal Wake Up Headphones.

The trick is that your personal headphones won't just nudge you into consciousness, they'll startle you into absolute panic. It's by no means a serene way to start the day, but with your heart fluttering and your nerves jangling there's no way you'll be dozing off again five minutes later.

But you must be a really sound sleeper to use these. If not, the ticking won't allow you to get to sleep in the first place!

珍道具

Dog Day Shoes
✳ ***Walk this way, and let the dog take the blame***

Wouldn't it be great if we could run as fast as dogs, we thought. Wouldn't it be even better if we had their ability to grip? But wouldn't it be best of all if we had shoes that left dog prints in the sand or in the mud rather than foot prints or shoe prints? Then we would be able to track through mud and onto carpets, over wet cement and onto glistening floors, and have everyone cursing some non-existent canine for the dirty deed. It's not a dog's life after all!

Diet Dishes

✳ *Satisfy your hunger with a culinary optical illusion*

We all know that the difficult thing about dieting is going without. Either you aren't able to eat the foods you want, or you have to eat less of them – either way you feel short changed. Not so much because your stomach gripes but because your brain isn't getting what it's used to.

Con it with Diet Dishes, which enable you to serve up full portions of your favourite foods while only consuming half the quantity. It's half as many calories, half the cost and half the dining time. Seems like magic? It's all done with mirrors.

Pet Slimming Bowls
✳ *Cuts calories without cries*

Cat too fat? Dog a hog? Monkey getting chunky? Pet Slimming Bowls, the animal version of the Diet Dishes, work just as well as their human counterparts. It's not often that a dog will acknowledge it has over-eaten but the tell-tale signs will soon become apparent.

If your clever canine knows he's been duped and howls until you give him another portion, don't fret – all that crying is bound to burn off some mutt gut.

Smearless Lip Stencil
✳ Kiss goodbye to smudged edges

Rushed, riled and unrested, a busy woman needs all the help she can get making herself beautiful in a hurry. The Smearless Lip Stencil is a fool-proof way to get your lipstick where it belongs: that's not on your teeth or on your chin, but on your lips.

But make sure your stencil is custom made. What makes one lovely lady beautiful could leave another wishing she'd opted for the natural look.

Kissing Coffee Cup

✴ **With such a sweet cup there's no need for sugar**

If you're not getting a big enough kick from your coffee, make it more stimulating – and more fun – with this turn-on of a coffee cup. After all, people crowd into coffee clubs not simply because the black liquid they pour is so much better than the home-made version – it's because of the atmosphere. So when a spoonful of instant and some hot water alone don't look like they're going to do it for you, try drinking your coffee from a Kissing Coffee Cup. It makes your coffee break a much sweeter occasion.

Pre-coloured Nails
✷ **Manicured fingernails the way you want them – in an instant**

Ladies, it can take ages to file, polish and dry your nails. You get them the way you want them, go out dancing for the evening and come home only to realize you'll be wearing a different colour outfit the next day. Time to start all over again!

But not if you have a few sets of Pre-coloured Nails which can be switched at a moment's notice. No mess, no polish, no continual expense, and they're small enough for extra sets to be taken along in a handbag – just in case. The only quicker way to change your nail colour is to stick your fingers in a bucket of paint.

Backward Print Pads

* **Shoes with soles that keep your secret**

     Shoes are a dead give-away about who we are and where we're heading. This basic flaw in footwear design can literally be turned to the advantage of the savvy spy, or wary walker, with Backward Print Pads. These second soles that attach to the bottoms of your shoes send would-be assailants in completely the wrong direction.

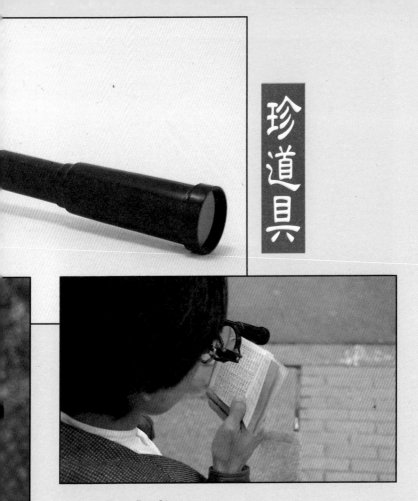

珍道具

Near Far Glasses

✳ See what's up close and way in the distance...at the same time

The telescope/microscope lenses of Near Far Glasses allow the wearer simultaneously to see both fine detail and objects on the horizon, eradicating the need to shift focus. You can read the fine print in your book while you wait for a taxi and scout for taxis streets away at the same time. Without adjusting your gaze, you can see the tiny markings on your map and check them against the landmarks that surround you.

Polish Pump
✳ For dry nails – quick

Waiting for nails to dry seems to take forever. And, while you're waiting, if you accidentally brush them against something they'll have to be redone. Complete immobility isn't much fun.

To speed things up use the Polish Pump. Squeeze the air ball with one hand and the five tubes each direct a stream of air directly onto the five fingernails of your other hand.

You might ask, why not simply connect the tubes to an electric fan? Well, this way, one of your hands always has something to do. The time will just whizz by.

Selective Alarm Clock

* Only wakes the person who needs waking

The problem with alarm clocks is that they make too much noise. While that's fine for the person who wants to get up, it's not so great for those who'd like to keep on sleeping. It's especially difficult for large families and for husbands who want to sneak out and hit a few rounds of golf before their wives tell them that the car needs mending.

The Selective Alarm Clock is the solution. With its sound proof acrylic box and personal headphone attachment, this way the bell tolls only for the person who set the timer.

Portable Countryside

✳ If you can't take the country out of the boy, let him carry a bit around town

Big cities mean intimidating, towering skyscrapers and a puzzling maze of subways. Worst of all is the lack of natural sights and smells. Armed with a personal Portable Countryside the simple farm boy or born again naturalist need never feel too urban when weaving their way through the concrete jungle. From now on, the walk to work or school will always be pleasantly scenic and familiar.

We recommend using the backstreets whenever possible. Exposure to exhaust fumes will kill your plants.

Commuter's Fast Pass

✳ *Flash with panache*

How many times have your fumbling fingers struggled to take off your gloves, fish out your pass and put it away again on cold mornings? And, sometimes, when you can't find it, the people behind you grow impatient. Frankly, it's embarrassing.

Consider the Commuter's Fast Pass for a quick in and out. For your convenience and comfort a see-through pocket for your commuting documents is attached to the outside of a warm woollen mitten. There's also a fingerless knit version for summer. An affected wave of the hand gets you through all the checkpoints and gives a certain air of chic to boot.

Since people on trains tend to stare at things, make sure your travel-pass photo is a good one.

珍道具

Traveller's Ice Pack
✴ The next best thing to staying at home in bed

When you have a fever or you're suffering from the world's worst hangover but you have to go out, wouldn't it be convenient if you could keep bundled up with a cold compress on your head until you get home again?

The Traveller's Ice Pack keeps your fever down while you do the town. It's slim, so you can walk down busy streets, and adjustable, so you can use it while riding trains or sitting at your desk. And if you're really ill, nothing beats it for making the trip to the chemist bearable.

The best part is that it's extremely noticeable: just what you need to illicit tons of sympathy from your friends and colleagues.

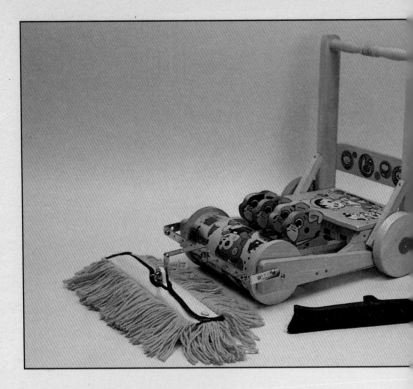

Cling Clang Cleaner

✳ *Put your child's love of toys to a more practical use*

Every parent who loves to sleep will attest unhappily to the fact that little children who have just learned how to walk love to show off their new skill. They 'cling clang' with their toys as soon as the sun comes up.

But don't discourage youthful exuberance, channel it to good use. The Cling Clang Cleaner is a lovable child's toy with attachments that also make it a mop or broom. This way, even though your child wakes you from sound slumber, at least the house will be sparking. If it's still in one piece.

Self-airing Shoes
✴ Furthers the fight against foot odour

Athlete's foot thrives in dark wet places. Fight fungus by keeping your socks dry and your shoes ventilated with Self-airing Shoes. Offending germs can neither rest nor reproduce as every step pumps a stream of wind through the shoe. You'll smell better and enjoy the sensation of walking on air.

Look out for embarrassing noises.

Scrub Gloves

✳ Twelve times the power to scour

The removal of stubborn stains from dirty pots and pans requires sturdy gloves, several sponges, scouring brushes, and a lot of elbow grease. Why not keep all these elements together in one place, ready for action? Cut down on washing time and effort with Scrub Gloves. Your grip will be a little restricted, so take care when handling your clean crockery or you may find your gloves will also reduce the number of dishes you own.

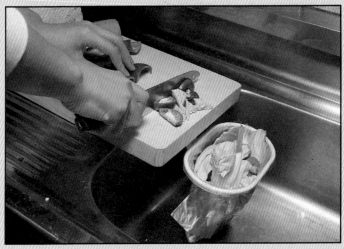

Chopping Block Litter Bag

✳ **Make your chopping block a trash-free zone**

When you're chopping in the kitchen valuable space is taken up by rubbish that isn't destined to become dinner.

What you need is a rubbish bag right next to the cutting board. Bin those bones, sling those shells and veto that vegetable waste. Instant elimination means no clutter in the cutting area and no trash mixed back in with the food.

When the time comes to clear away the mess, throwing out the chopping refuse is a snap.

Baby Walking Slippers

✳ First steps need a helping hand...and two supporting feet

Wh**hen babies learn to walk they spend a lot of time face down on the floor while their feet get used to the habit of walking. Baby Walking Slippers are designed to minimize the time and the stumbling required before your wee one gets his legs.

Velcro tabs attached to his little soles cling to the tops of the parent's slippers and, one-two, one-two, the child cuts through all those trial and error trip-u-lations and learns the technique straight from an expert.

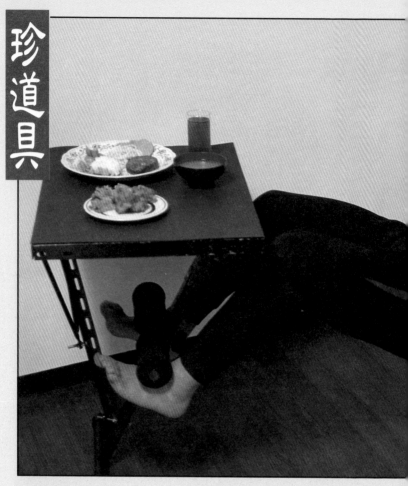

珍道具

Sit-up Table
✳ Take off calories while you take in calories

The most common excuse for not exercising is 'I can't find the time.' It's impossible to make that claim if you have a Sit-up Table. Now, while you're chewing you can also be crunching.

Beginners may want to start with just one sit-up every two to three bites, but advanced users will soon be able to squeeze off several exercises per mouthful.

If you're really lucky all that motion while you're trying to eat will result in a total loss of appetite. What could be better?

Shuffling/Scrubbing Shoes

✳ *Tidy your tiles while you cut a rug*

Most people like clean, but they don't like cleaning. Step into some Shuffling/Scrubbing Shoes and all you need do is stroll around your home and your floors will sparkle. Shuffle backwards, shuffle forwards, maybe even pretend you're skating. Then hose off the suds and enjoy a squeaky clean home.

You'll soon find that dancing is the best way to remove stubborn stains from the bathroom or kitchen and that your Shuffling/ Scrubbing Shoes are the best way to get the job done. But exercise caution. It's hard enough to stand in these things, let alone disco. An unintentional spill in these could give break dancing a whole new meaning.

Good Posture Seat

✳ Straighten out your employees

Desks have a tendency to bring out the worst in a person's posture. When seated at their desks, some people constantly kick the legs of the table, some lean back like they're on holiday, and others tap their feet to music that's playing in their head. The Good Posture Seat puts a stop to all this fun and nonsense.

Sit down in one of these and you'll soon get the idea. With your spine pressed firmly into the back of the chair and your feet flat on the floor there'll be no more napping. Just imagine how much more productive you'll be.

Best of all, good habits die hard. Staff will often outlive their chairs.

Shiatsu Shoes

＊ For adults who like massage and children who like to step on people

In a household where everyone works hard, plays hard and comes home beat, it's difficult to find someone willing to massage your tired body. At the end of a long day only the kids have any energy left, but children don't know a thing about massage. Thanks to Shiatsu Shoes they don't have to.

Shiatsu Shoes have ten ringed plastic platforms on either sole. With a fifty-pound child, that means five pounds of direct pressure from each ring every time the small one lifts a foot. Since small children are notoriously unable to keep still, the rings will vibrate with every step, providing soothing relief for tired adults.

Bear in mind that your little masseuse may not have the cleanest shoes around. Always check their soles first or you may wind up with more on your back than you bargained for.

Portable Lamp Post
✳ *You'll never walk down a dark street again*

It's often not safe to be out at night, especially when you're a woman walking poorly lit streets. You know you shouldn't venture away from bright areas, but sometimes you just have to go down a dark road.

The Portable Lamp Post gives you an edge against potential attack from shadow-dwellers. It's bright and it's big and makes a loud clattering noise. If the light doesn't deter your attacker, the noise will.

Just two drawbacks. Immensely useful when the sun goes down, it's a pain to lug around in the daytime. And, hanging around under a lamp post may lead to you being mistaken for an enterprising prostitute.

Pet Pick-up

✳ It's time dogs and cats cleaned up after themselves

○mall animals are cute, but they're also messy. Apart from the smell and the noise there's also all that hair they leave behind them.

Hence the need for the Pet Pick-up. It lets the offending animal clear up its own debris almost in the same instant it's deposited. As long as the owner remembers to tear off the soiled outer sheet every now and then, the pet leaves a clean trail wherever it goes – with the added bonus of picking up human bits of trash too.

Your pets won't like it much at first, but they'll soon become as attached to it as they are to their own shadow.

珍道具

Ladies' Leg Guard

✳ **Now fashion and foul weather go together**

You've been splashed by passing vehicles one time too many. The Ladies' Leg Guard is designed especially for ladies who don't have the necessary dodging skills. They know best that stockings don't recover from muddy splatters the way an unclad leg responds to a quick wipe down. So, just attach one of these Leg Guards to the hem of your skirt and let the weather do its worst.

Self-Lighting Cigarettes
✳ *Neither wind nor rain will stop a smoke lighting again – they're match attached*

Now smokers needn't pat their pockets frantically, poke their heads into explosive gas ranges, or rub sticks together in a feeble attempt to get a light. With Self-Lighting Cigarettes the match is built in. This brilliant idea might also work for candles and fireworks, in fact anything that needs lighting.

The convenience far outweighs the discomfort of inhaling all the sulphur and gunpowder that's part of the match head.

Chattering Chewer

✳ *Mashes up your meal so you don't have to*

Anthropologists tell us that our jaws are weaker today than they used to be. Tools like scissors and pliers have become substitutes for teeth, and the consumption of lots of processed food has decreased our power to devour.

One solution is to exercise the mouth more – one two, chew chew – but an easier alternative is just to go full force in the other direction and avoid anything that might give our infirm incisors trouble.

The Chattering Chewer accomplishes this nicely. By squeezing it a few times, the dentally deficient diner can crush up those hard bits before attempting to ingest them on his own. Great for people who have problems with nuts and bones.

No-slip Stair Scoops

✳ On rainy days, don't go anywhere without a pair

Even at the best of times it's pretty tough climbing those slippery marble or stone stairs that certain designers relish erecting. But try mounting them on a rainy day and it's next to impossible. Why flirt with disaster?

Stair Scoops are made with a no-slip rubbery edge, not just on the part that connects with your foot, but also on the bottom so they won't slide off the stair. Just put one down ahead of each step and you can ascend with mounting confidence.

Either Way Slippers

✳ Slippers that slip right on

At the end of a long day, how good does it feel to slip into your slippers? At Japanese restaurants you can kick off your shoes and walk into a pair without even having to bend down: the hostess does the stooping and she makes sure the slippers are facing the right way. But at home there always seems to be a stubborn one that you have to kick around the room before you can get it facing the right way and get it on. Either Way Slippers put an end to this nuisance. No matter which way you step out of them when you're getting into your shoes in the morning, they'll always be facing in the right direction for you to step into them again when you get home.

Face Iron

✳ **Iron out the rough spots**

Ladies, have you ever happened to glance at your face in the bathroom mirror in the middle of the day and notice a huge mountain of foundation congealed in one spot? There's no need to scream. Just pull out your Face Iron and smooth it down.

The Face Iron won't take away your wrinkles, but it will uncrease the make-up that you put over them. In the same way that a brick layer wipes away the excess cement, you can level off your face.

Later in the afternoon, watch yourself when you're tempted to open your mouth in a wide laugh. Your face will crack.

Lip Stamp
✱ Pucker lips in a hurry

Lipstick has its plusses, but it takes far too long to apply. You have to rub it on, smear it into place, wipe off the excess. Provided you have one that matches the size of your mouth, the Lip Stamp will get the stuff on more quickly and look just as good. It only has to take a second to achieve rich colourful lips.

The only problem is that it takes a little bit longer to get the colour onto the stamp – you have to rub it on, smear it into place, wipe off the excess...

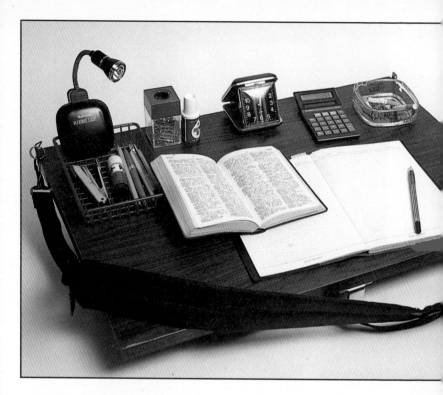

Anywhere Office

✳ *Wherever you are, take your desk with you*

In a competitive working environment there are people who get in to the office early, leave late, and take lunch at their desks just to stay one step ahead of the crowd. With the Anywhere Office there's no longer a need to complain that there just aren't enough hours in the day. There are plenty — you just need to use them right.

Now you can run errands, go to meetings, take business trips and even go out to eat without ever having to leave your desk.

245

Summer Suit Shorts
✳ *Being a businessman needn't mean being uncomfortable*

If you're a 'suit type' you'll find yourself staring longingly at kids in tank tops and cut-offs on long hot summer days, only able to console yourself and dismiss your sweaty discomfort with thoughts of your hefty pay cheque. When it comes to comfort, it seems the have-nots often have much more.

But now you can have the best of both worlds. By slipping into a pair of these trousers you can be as cool and comfortable as the beach bums. Fold them down just before you enter the office and your colleagues will be none the wiser as to your personal air conditioning.

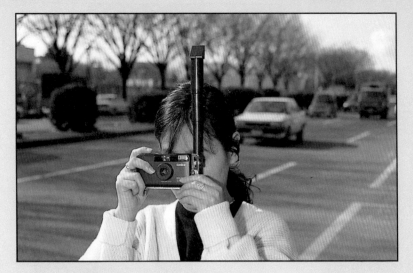

Rear View Camera

✳ *See ahead of you with one eye, behind you with the other*

Whilen you look through your viewfinder to compose the perfect picture postcard, you see the world as a flat entity, already developed, trimmed and pasted into your photo album. Unfortunately, the people around you don't share in your freeze-frame detachment from reality. There's always the danger that the last picture you ever take will be of your subject screaming you a warning just before you're flattened by a bus.

The periscope on this Rear View Camera eliminates this fear. No more turning away in the middle of your camera adjustments to verify that there aren't any approaching hazards. A quick glance with your rear eye is all it takes.

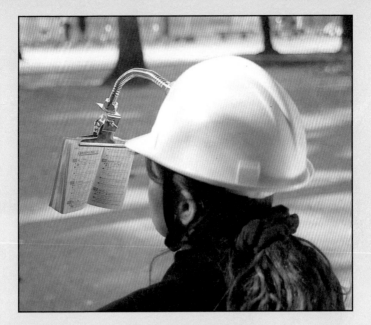

Hold-it Helmet

✴ **Keep two eyes on your valuables, twenty-four hours a day**

Big, bulky pieces of hard plastic that protect the head are very useful, but they leave tons of unexploited space. Why settle for just a helmet when it could do so much more?

With a metallic arm and clamp attached out in front you'll discover just how useful a helmet can be. It can hold your book on a crowded train, hold your pass when you're going through the station exit, even hold your camera when you want to take a picture. Helmet-top technology is still in its infancy. We've scarcely scratched the surface.

Self-Portrait Camera Stick
Do it yourself without the palaver

If you're travelling alone or as a couple, it's hard to get pictures with you in them. It can be embarrassing to have to ask someone to take the photo for you, confusing if they don't speak your language, even costly if the third party regards your camera as a gift!

With a fifty-seven-centimetre telescoping pole your dilemma is over. Expanding to three times its length for a full shot of you, your companion and your environs, your only problem will be that all your shots will capture you in the act of holding the pole. This could become a tiresome feature of your photo album – unless you really like poles.

Cigarette Joints

✳ **Now chain smokers can live up to their name**

Don't get the wrong idea about our Cigarette Joints. They're not a new type of herbal cigarette. They're joining rings to make the old ones last longer.

When smokers gripe that their cigarette breaks aren't long enough, maybe what they really need are longer cigarettes. Cut the filters off a few extra smokes, use your Cigarette Joints to attach them to the one in your mouth, and you'll have a super-sized cigarette guaranteed to fulfil even your worst cravings.

Magnifying Fork

✳ When it looks more, you'll eat less

If the remaining sliver of cake is too small or the portions allowed by your diet too intolerably tiny, use a Magnifying Fork or the companion Expander Spoon and see more, sense more, taste more.

Tests show that nibbles eaten with the Magnifying Fork can be more satisfying than those had without, but much depends on one's state of mind. Sceptics tend to leave the table frustrated and unfulfilled. Gullible folk swear by it.

Swiss Army Gloves

✳ **Multi-purpose mittens that keep you ready for anything**

Those clever Swiss Army officers put a compass, screwdriver and nail clippers onto a pocket knife and revolutionized the average blade. Not to be caught bringing up the rear, the Americans have done similar things with flashlights that double as radios, and the Japanese have worked wonders with watches and calculators.

But it took the Art of Chindogu to realize that the tools very few humans ever hazard to leave behind are their hands.

Swiss Army Gloves provide a lighter, fork, corkscrew, bottle opener, pen, cutter, hole puncher and two screwdrivers all at the tips of your fingers – literally.

Skeeter Slippers
✳ **Knock 'em dead wherever you tread**

Those light-it-and-leave-it mosquito repellents work fine in the home. They smell nice and keep the pests away. But that won't keep the little blighters at bay if you have to go outside.

Try Skeeter Slippers. There's nothing to carry, nothing to spray and you wear the insect coils at foot level so that the rising smoke covers your entire body. Walk confidently through grass and next to streams: the mosquitoes simply won't bother you. And you'll be popular wherever you go because you'll carry your bug free environment with you.

Shirtless Sleeves

✱ A change of shirt you can keep in your pocket

The downside of being an extremely successful business-person is the huge cleaning bill. Every day you have to put on a freshly-laundered shirt just so it can peek out from the sleeves of your jacket. Your boss notices very little apart from your back and hands at the keyboard, so why go to so much trouble? All that cleaning seems like a waste of time and money.

Why not try some Shirtless Sleeves? A good set of twenty or so can be stored in a briefcase and easily washed out in the sink. Clean sleeves every day and no one but you need know how long it's been since you last washed your shirt.

The Walls Have Eyes

✳ Perform under scrutiny – somebody's watching you

There's only one good substitute for self-discipline and that's the discipline inflicted by others. Too often students spend the whole day dreading the work ahead of them, then, when the rest of the world has gone to bed, they fidget, drift and eventually fall asleep.

That's why this screen of a hundred eyes is so useful. Pull it down when you finally want to get down to business and the power of these relentless stares and glares will keep you alert and concentrated.

Recommended only for study areas, though. This screen can be unnerving when placed in the bathroom or bedroom.

Precise Pacer

✳ *Accurate measurements that others can duplicate*

Counting off paces to measure distances works up to a point. But when those same steps are paced off again, there's often a different result – even when the same person does the pacing. The length of space between steps always varies and is hard to control.

That's why the Precise Pacer is so convenient. Strap one of these to your ankles and every step you take will measure the same. Forget centimetres, metres and kilometres, with the Precise Pacer you can make accurate assessments of your own.

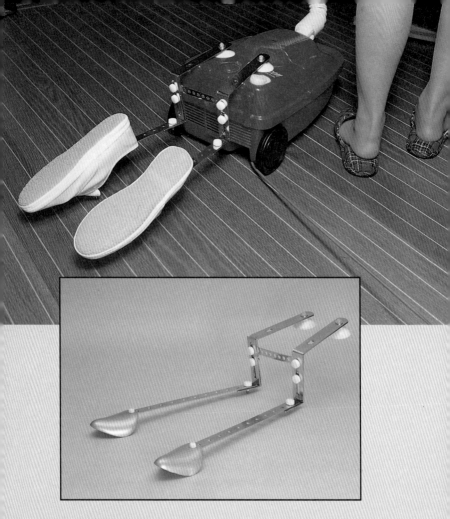

Vacuum Ventilator

✳ Hoover the house and freshen your footwear...at the same time

Vacuum cleaners don't just suck, they blow. A steady stream of clean filtered air, warmed by the motor, is expelled from the rear and escapes to the ceiling. Harness this resource and use it to air your tennis shoes.

Shoes moist with perspiration or the remains of a rainy day should be placed onto the Vacuum Ventilator and by the time the floors are clean, your shoes will be fresh, dry and ready to wear.

Plateless Placemats

✳ Enjoy the sight of a table full of dishes, but avoid the washing up

Ho w often have you laid out cookies, rolls, sandwiches, nuts and hard boiled eggs on an array of pretty plates and dainty dishes only to wind up washing away three crumbs and an oil spot at the end of your meal and wondering why you bothered?

More than once? Then try Plateless Placemats. While permitting the elegant presentation of food, they save time, trouble and resources when it comes to cleaning up. With a single wipe or shake they are as good as new and, since they're double-sided, every now and then you can simply flip them over and treat yourself to the good china.

It's worth remembering that if you're having soup or stew for dinner, you'll need to make other arrangements.

Umbrella Brush

✷ When washing the ceiling doesn't mean washing your hair

Bathrooms are a breeding ground for mould and fungi. To make them easier to clean, a scrubbing brush attached to a hose means that a steady stream of water will wash away all the nasty stuff once you've loosened it from the tiles.

But what about the ceiling? That gets dirty, too. But you don't want all that murky water raining down on your head. That's why we routed the stream through rain's greatest enemy. The umbrella.

Don't be superstitious about opening your brolly in the house, or you'll get very wet.

Stroll 'n' Style

✳ Strut your stuff while you do your do

If *Saturday Night Fever*'s Tony Monero had had one of these, the movie would have been ten minutes shorter. With the Stroll 'n' Style, you don't need to spend precious time in front of the mirror with a hair drier every morning. Just slip this contraption on and off you go to work.

Every step you take will send a jet of air through your freshly washed head of hair; drying, styling, but requiring no extra time, energy or electricity.

Great for people with commutes that include long stretches of walking. Not as effective if you drive or take the bus.

Deep Fry Spatter Shield

✳ Cook the goods and keep your distance

The taste, the sound, the smell of fried food is wonderful – everything's great, except the feel of it. If you're hit in the arm with a splash of oil, the pain will usually last longer than your dinner.

The Deep Fry Spatter Shield welcomes you to the new world of deep frying. Behind the safety of its clear plastic, you can not only see what you're doing but you're protected from those painful pops when the bits hit the pan. There's even a pair of chopsticks attached so you can load another piece of food in safety and with ease. If you're brave enough, you can even stick your face right in front of it and enjoy watching the droplets accumulate harmlessly on the other side.

Tear-free Onion Chopper

✳ Cutting onions is no longer something to cry about

$\mathbb{C}$hopping onions while holding back the tears is an age-old problem which is long overdue a remedy. Tissues are the obvious answer but, prevention being better than cure, an acrylic box with a big knife inside gets our vote.

The Tear-free Onion Chopper allows you to slice all you want without having to worry about eye-irritating odours and fumes. It's so safe, your child can help out in the kitchen and you won't need to fret over cut fingers.

It takes a little practice to cut an onion without holding it, but because you're not distracted by tears any more the job gets done in

next to no time. And, ladies, the happy chopper now has more time to spend crying her eyes out in front of the afternoon soap operas.

Leg-up Lounger

✳ Because leaning is easier than standing

Washing dishes, cooking, ironing – these are tedious and tiring chores that are hard to do sitting down. But with a Leg-up Lounger you no longer have to be on your feet all day.

Like the crane or the ostrich, who alternate feet so they don't get too tired, busy people can relieve half their load by using this cushioned leg rest attached to a collapsible tripod. At the end of the day, you'll feel like you've been sitting down half the time.

Use two and you'll feel like you've been sitting down all the time, but that would be greedy and just a little unstable.

Ear Extender

✳ *Forget batteries and wires, hear a crisp new sound*

Who says that the humble, hand-crafted Art of Chindogu can't compete with the mass-produced technological wonders being churned out by those electronic manufacturing giants? The Ear Extender is a sturdily built, water-resistant, battery-free hearing aid that's virtually fool-proof and guaranteed to work whatever the circumstances. No transistors to fiddle with, no cells to charge, and you'll never have to worry about losing these down the drain!

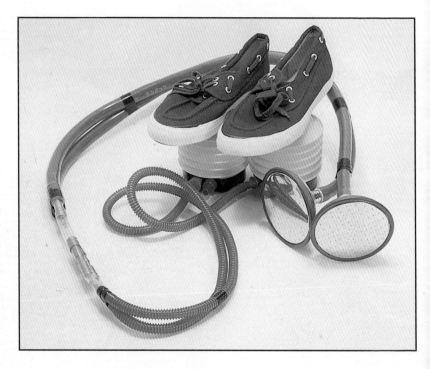

Bubble Bath Runner

✳ Soak your muscles in sweat, and then in the bath

Jogging on the spot keeps a body in shape, but what about all that energy exerted in the process? It usually goes to waste. This innovative gadget gives new meaning to the term 'running a bath'. Sprinkle in a little bath foam, slip into the Bubble Bath Runner shoes and you can create a cosy, sudsy paradise for escaping into once you've worked up a healthy sweat.

Alternatively, use it to give someone you love a whirlpool bath. And then it's your turn to relax in the tub while they get grimy again returning the favour.

Desk Dreamer's Chin Rest

✳ Eaten too much for lunch? Had one beer too many? Catch a quick nap at your desk

Yes, we all know that, officially, you're not supposed to sleep in the office but you could argue that a cat nap will enhance your afternoon performance. How many working hours get wasted because people become jaded as the day wears on? How many employees would be saved from going home early because they feel 'out of it'? That's why this Chindogu for the chin is so handy. You don't get comfortable enough to snooze through the whole afternoon, but you do get a rest and without the stiff neck and ink smears on the forehead that can result from sleeping atop the desk proper.

And there's no need to fear about talking in your sleep – since the weight of the head rests on the jaw, your colleagues will enjoy perfect peace and quiet.

Infant Pleasing Camera

✳ Makes all of baby's pictures pleasant

You can scream, wave your hands, jump up and down and call your child's name cajolingly, but all too often you'll still wind up with pictures of the poor kid crying. Change the theme of your photo album from frightened to fun with the Infant Pleasing Camera. And stop making a fool of yourself.

Just whip it out, blow on the mouthpiece and wiggle the box. Colourful snakes and streamers come to life to grab your child's attention while you grab a photo. They'll even look like they were enjoying the visit to the museum.

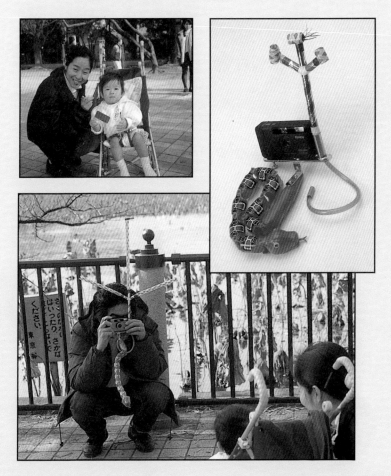

✳ *Zooming without the blooming expense*

The miracle of photography isn't in the camera, it's in the film. But that's not what the manufacturers would have you believe. They want you to think that to take good pictures you need costly peripherals like timers, zoom lenses and auto focusing. Well, we say 'ha' to that and have designed a gadget that echoes our sentiments.

The Scenic Extender will take you several metres closer to your subject without any expensive equipment. You can even use a disposable camera. Just squeeze the bulb and snap the picture.

Look out for our technological rivals' new top-of-the-range camera that flies, available soon in shops near you.

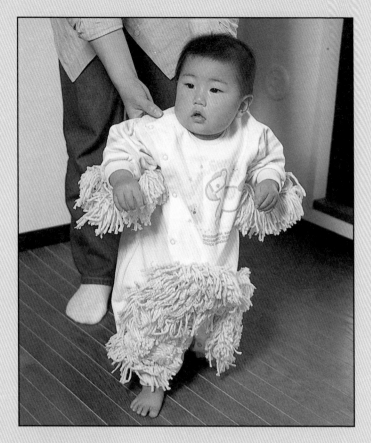

Baby Mops

✳ *Make your children work for their keep*

After the birth of a child there's always the temptation to say 'Yes, it's cute, but what can it do?' Until recently the answer was simply 'lie there and cry', but now babies can be put on the payroll, so to speak, almost as soon as they're born.

Just dress your young one in Baby Mops and set him or her down on any hard wood or tile floor that needs cleaning. You may at first need to get things started by calling to the infant from across the room, but pretty soon they'll be doing it all by themselves.

There's no child exploitation involved. The kid is doing what he does best anyway: crawling. But with Baby Mops he's also learning responsibility and a healthy work ethic.

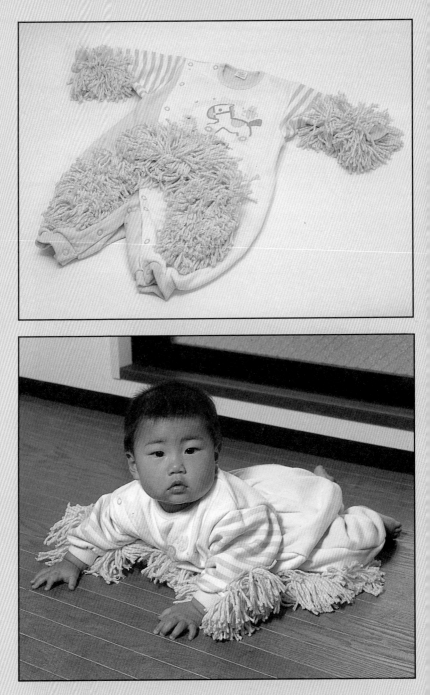

TV for One

✳ Keep your television habits to yourself

A television can be an annoying presence to those who aren't watching it (or who are trying not to watch it). The light flickers, the movement distracts, the subjects on the screen vie with your needlepoint for your attention. You could invest in a new Personal-size TV, but they're about as much fun to watch as candlelight bouncing off a postage stamp.

Better by far is a TV for One. The unit – complete with twenty-one-inch screen – allows one person to enjoy their favourite show while another sleeps or does their homework. Adults can also enjoy sleazy night-time programmes while protecting the morals of young ones who aren't yet old enough to view said trash.

Umbrella Bell
✳ *Ring your thing to get past fast*

There's only one thing harder than moving through a crowd of sluggish Sunday strollers: moving through the same crowd on a rainy day. Umbrellas slow pedestrian traffic to a crawl.

Ever noticed how everyone jumps out of the way when a cyclist sounds his bell? That's the idea behind this umbrella attachment. Give it a ring whenever you need some space and by the time the others notice you're just another lowly stroller, they've already cleared the way.

Contact Lens Protectors

✳ Never lose a lens again

Exercise, wind, tears – all these things can make a contact lens pop out without warning. When this happens it's unlikely you'll ever find it: it's small, colourless, and you can only see well out of one eye to look for it.

With the Contact Lens Protector you always know where the missing lens is. In your Protector! No more hours wasted on your hands and knees groping in vain. No more disquieting crunches when someone approaches to ask what you're looking for. No more eviction notices after you use your rent money to buy yet another new lens.

Our Contact Lens Protectors keep lenses, lashes, and even glass eyes in front of your face at all times.

Picture Protector

✴ Keeps creeps from sneaking into your shots

Elvis Presley was notorious for picture crashing. He'd lean into a scene, unbeknown to the photographer or the subject, and when they got their film developed they'd be all shook up. But since it's unlikely that the King is available for more unscheduled photo shoots, the Picture Protector should be all you need.

With two cords that attach to the sides of the photographer and the subject an impassable fortress is created. For total idiots – who either don't see the string or think it's a finish line – each cord is also equipped with a sign that says 'Picture Taking in Progress'.

Mirror-bottom Wash Basin
✳ See your face as you're washing it

Sound obvious? Think about it. You don't really look at your face as you're washing, do you? Chances are you glance up at a mirror between washes. That may be the way it's always been, but it doesn't have to be this way in future.

Ladies especially can verify their make-up is coming off by watching as they're washing. The Mirror-bottom Wash Basin may well be the most effective face cleaning tool since the invention of water.

Drawbacks? Well, as you scrub, the water in the basin tends to cloud up, causing the user's face to fade out in front of their eyes. This can be alarming.

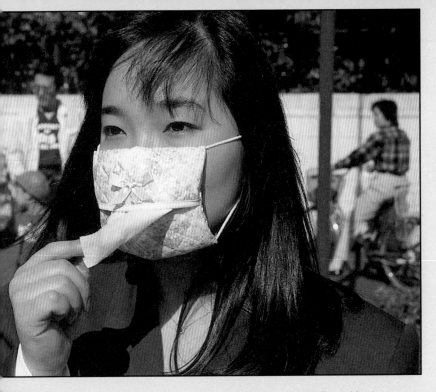

Tissue-equipped Face Mask

✳ *A Kleenex container that's fast, fashionable, and right where you need it*

Some people wear masks when they suffer from hay fever. Put your mask to greater use by making it serve as an appropriately associated tissue holder too. Not only do Tissue-equipped Face Masks turn the pale white gauze numbers into something that keeps the wearer beautiful even though she's sick, they also add an extra barrier against the offending pollen: a large pile of tissues.

When the mask runs low on tissues, the wearer starts sniffling more and she knows it's time to top up her Kleenex.

珍道具

Stay-in-place Sleeper
✳ The immobilizing mattress for middle of the night movers

Toss and turn when you're not sleeping well? Wiggling your covers and flinging your legs out of the bed are often manifestations of deeper troubles. The Stay-in-place Sleeper stops you from getting out of hand and from vacating your spot in the bed.

Slip into your niche when you lie down at night and the chances are you'll still be there in the morning. It's particularly useful for married couples who kick each other and wrestle over the sheets.

If you wake to find yourself on top of a pile of foam rubber – your Sleeper torn to shreds – this Chindogu probably isn't for you.

Umbrella Hat

✳ *Look! No hands!*

People with packages, shoppers with shopping bags, or sightseers on strolls who just don't want to have to hold an umbrella up all the time: these are just a few of the folk who stand to benefit from the Umbrella Hat. No more accidentally jabbing people with your umbrella. And your arms are unencumbered to protect yourselves against jabs from others!

So it's a little less attractive when the sun comes out and you've got a closed umbrella sticking out of your head. But the merits of this handy headwear are otherwise endless.

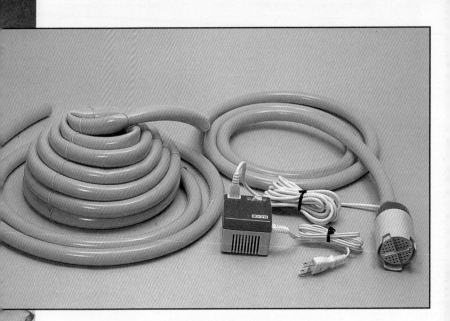

Auto-cycling Cool Compress

✳ **Keep your fever down with a pampering pump**

An ice pack or towel soaked in cold water is quite the best thing to bring a fever down. Within seconds these remedies start to cool your forehead, but said forehead also tends to heat up said instruments, necessitating frequent replacements. Blast those pesky laws of physics.

The Auto-cycling Cool Compress prevents you or your kindly caretaker from constantly having to run for more cold water. Just wrap the hose around your head and stick the pump in a bucket of water. As the cool liquid circulates, your fever is eased and the heat is carried back to the bucket. The sickly victim's benefits are endless: fever relief, a head and face massage, plus a low-pitched womb-like pulsing to lull him or her to sleep and aid fast recovery.

It's such a great feeling – watch out for hypochondriacs.

Environment Friendly Mosquito Nets

✳ *The easy, economical and ecologically sound way to keep bugs at bay*

In the summer months you might feel the need to erect huge tents of netting to keep the bugs out. You might even end up poisoning your own environment and polluting every breath of air just to kill a few tiny insects. Since the bugs are only going to bite the parts of your body they can get to, cover those and you've solved the problem!

The Environment Friendly Mosquito Net set comes with a face cover and bags for each hand and foot. Slip these on, make sure those flaps in your pyjamas are closed tightly, and you won't have a problem with the bugs the whole night.

Don't get a fright when you catch a glimpse of yourself in the bathroom mirror in the middle of the night! And when you wake up the next morning and shed the netting, watch out for some pretty hungry mosquitoes.

Portable Parking Spot

✳ Have space, will park

Victims of our socialization, a tiny white outline with a car inside is perceived to be a parking space. A large open area with no white line is not a parking space. The Portable Parking Spot allows you to turn this misconception to your own benefit. Simply roll the white painted strip around your car when you arrive and pick it up on your way out. Note: this last part tends to annoy other drivers if they're waiting to move in after you.

There's no need to worry about traffic wardens ticketing you. Suffering from the same disease of socialization, they seldom think to check the white line to verify that it really is a parking space and not simply a strip of paper that some clever person has brought with them.

Grin Grabber

Forces even the crankiest folk to crack a smile

Doctors have noticed that people who smile frequently get fewer wrinkles and tend to have healthier skin. The irony is that by the time a doctor tells you this, you've already started to lose your looks and so have nothing to smile about.

The Grin Grabber solves this problem. Slip it on, stick the hooks into either side of your mouth, and pull the cord. It's guaranteed to correct a scowl. And it's economical, too. Just one person wearing this gadget is sure to get an entire room grinning madly.

Drive-by Drier

✴ Air your attire while you tour the town

Now the natural feel and aroma of garments drip-dried in the great outdoors is easily achievable in the same time it takes to choose a drying cycle on your washing machine. You also get the luxury of choosing which section of town you want to smell like.

The Drive-by Drier renders a full load of laundry wearable in just twenty minutes on the highway, twenty-five in the city. (Estimates based on Tokyo test drives; actual drying time may vary.)

Geisha On The Go

✳ *No time left to put on your make-up? Take a bow and you're ready to rock*

The evolution of cosmetic particle application has finally taken an intelligent turn. The powder goes on at quantum speed – with one quick dip. And you don't even need a mirror; missing a spot with Geisha On The Go would be like going swimming and not getting wet.

Anyone desiring information on how to join the
International Chindogu Academy
may write to:

Kenji Kawakami
Chindogu Academy
5–12–12 Koishikawa
Bunkyo-Ku
Tokyo 113
Japan

or on e-mail at: http://www.chindogu.com

or care of
HarperCollins*Publishers*
77–85 Fulham Palace Road
London W12 8JB